Lackawanna Railroad

In Color

VOLUME 2

by

Jeremy F. Plant

To access our full library *In Color* visit us at
www.morningsunbooks.com

Published by
Morning Sun Books, Inc.
9 Pheasant Lane
Scotch Plains, NJ 07076
Printed in Korea

Library of Congress
Catalog Card No. 90-061261

First Printing
ISBN 1-58248-108-3

ROBERT J. YANOSEY, President

Acknowledgements

First and foremost, I want to thank the photographers whose work appears on these pages: Arthur Angstadt, Henry G. Becker, Steve Bogen, Dr. C. K. Botkin, Robert Chamberlin, Marvin H. Cohen, Robert F. Collins, William Echternacht, William Ellis, R. Fillman, Ted Gay, Theodore Gleichmann, Jr., W. T. Greenberg, E. P. Griffith, Steve Hepler, Al Holtz, Bill Hopping, Norman E. Kohl, Frank C. Kozempel, George Leilich, Joseph McCarthy, William McChesney, Edward Miller, Arthur Mitchell, Charles E. Nagle, Charles Parsons, Henry W. Peterson, Paul Reynolds, James P. Shuman, Richard Solomon, Frank Watson, J. J. Wheelihan, J. J. Young, and William Young. Mike Del Vecchio, W. T. Greenberg, Pat Lederer, the Hawk Mountain Chapter of the National Railway Historical Society, the Don Ball Collection, and Mark Schmidt graciously shared material from their collections. Robert Yanosey of Morning Sun Books provided encouragement and support to push the project to completion. Thanks to Brian D. Plant, who assisted in photo selection and layout, and to Mike Del Vecchio, without whose assistance and insight the book could not have been written. And finally, a word about Bob Yanosey and the work that goes into this and most other Morning Sun books. Few readers realize that most of the photographers featured in these books are located by and their works accessed through the efforts of Bob. His tireless energy in this regard has made these books possible and preserved the color work of here-to-fore unknown as well as more celebrated photographers. Thanks Bob, for digging this wonderful stuff out and making it available for all of us to enjoy!
Jeremy F. Plant
Hershey, Pennsylvania

Table of Contents

Above and Page 1 ▪ F3 #621A and two Train Masters are westbound through Denville, NJ in June 1958. *(Joseph McCarthy)*

My first exposure to the Lackawanna came in 1953, when my father took my brother Jeff and me on a short trip to New York's Southern Tier. We visited the Corning Glass Works, and stayed in a motel that gave us a nice opportunity to stroll the town and see some of the railroad action. The first glimpse of the PHOEBE SNOW, dazzling in its maroon and gray livery, was an unforgettable experience. The ERIE LIMITED was nice, too, and the New York Central stole the show after dark with a 2-8-2 doing some street running, as I recall. We headed up to see Letchworth Park, and again around Dansville had a nice view of the PHOEBE SNOW on its way east. Quite an introduction!

Living far from the nearest Lackawanna line – actually, it was only about 100 miles from Troy to Utica and Richfield Springs, the closest Lackawanna locations, but in those days distances were meaningful – I had to wait until well into the Erie Lackawanna era to sample action on the former Lackawanna lines in the three states in which it ran, New York, Pennsylvania, and New Jersey. Going to school at Colgate University gave me a chance to explore the line to Utica, which went within a few miles of the college, and the various lines around Binghamton. Later, courtesy of the U. S. Army and stationing at Fort Monmouth, New Jersey, I had a chance to get to know the New Jersey lines. By then, the EL had adopted the Lackawanna paint scheme for its diesels, and the DL&W seemed to live on in the beautiful three-color scheme of its successor road.

This book is an in-depth look at the Lackawanna. We begin the series with coverage of Lackawanna operations in the state of New Jersey, starting at the Hudson River and ending at the Delaware. In terms of distance, it's only about 100 miles as the crow flies, but within that space the DL&W managed to pack a great amount of railroad activity on a variety of lines. We start with a look at operations at waterside in Hoboken, follow the Morris & Essex west to Denville, then return to Hoboken for a trip over the parallel Boonton Line to its connection with the M&E at Denville. Continuing west, we explore the big centers of activity at Dover and Port Morris, then take sidetrips up the Sussex Branch and the Old Main before returning to Port Morris for the final miles of our trip to the Delaware Water Gap and the Commonwealth of Pennsylvania.

The second half of the book examines the Lackawanna in Pennsylvania and New York. Starting at the Delaware Water Gap, we have a tour of the cement district, climb the Poconos, look at the heart of Lackawanna operations in the city of Scranton, and head west to Buffalo, with a few side trips on the branches feeding in to the main line. The pictures have been chosen to give as good a feel as possible for the scenery, operations, motive power, and equipment of the railroad. A few post-merger shots are included, to help tell the full story of the railroad, but for the most part it's a trip back to the great years of the 1940s and 1950s, when the future of the Lackawanna still seemed bright, railroads were still the dominant mode of transportation, and the steam engine was gradually giving way to the diesel.

History

The history of the Lackawanna has several major themes: the competition between railroads and canals in the first half of the 19th century; the lucrative business in hard coal pouring down from the mines of Pennsylvania; the positioning of northern New Jersey as a logical entryway for railroads to reach the Greater New York metropolis; the consolidation through merger, lease, and acquisition of smaller roads into one single New York to Buffalo trunk line; and the movement of people, beginning in the 1880s, from the established cities around New York City to the suburbs in central New Jersey, at a time before the automobile when commuting meant travel to work by train.

The development of the anthracite mining industry in northeastern Pennsylvania in the first half of the 19th century was a great spur to the development of better transportation facilities, to move the vast amounts of coal eastward from the mines to consumers in the populated region along the Atlantic seaboard. The anthracite mining operations covered much of the mountainous territory between Scranton and Carbondale on the north, along the Susquehanna River; Pottsville on the Schuylkill, to the south and west; and Mauch Chunk (now Jim Thorpe) on the south and east. Within the broad triangle, there were distinct coal fields, each centered on one of the three river basins. However, none of the three rivers was navigable, and the Susquehanna headed in the wrong direction to provide a route to the major markets of the East Coast.

Anthracite mining started around the time of the great "canal craze" in the Northeast. The development of the Erie Canal in New York State signaled a revolution in transportation. The state created a highway of water that took advantage of its existing river system, the Hudson and its tributary the Mohawk, which provides a pathway leading easily to the Great Lakes from the Atlantic. New York had no anthracite coal to convey over the canal, but over it flooded the agricultural products of the West to the New York metropolitan region. The other states of the region saw its success and, geography notwithstanding, decided to emulate the Empire State. Of special importance to New Jersey was a water route between the Delaware River and New York harbor for the movement of coal. Such a route would be superior to the routing of coal on coastal vessels from the Port of Philadelphia to New York, and give New Jersey a major role in the new commerce, as well as providing competition for the Erie Canal in other east-west traffic.

The obvious route was across the waist of the state, from Philadelphia to New York, with the Raritan River providing much of the route. This route, however, required much of the anthracite to move far south of its point of origination before it moved eastward through the state. As new coalfields emerged around the Lackawanna River and Scranton, the need for a route across the northern part of New Jersey became more obvious. Geography, though, made a canal across northern New Jersey problematic. Western New Jersey is hilly, and the watersheds of the Delaware and Hudson rivers are separated by a line of ridges that necessitated a total rise and fall of over a thousand feet in elevation.

Such a path, though, was apparent, using the Musconetcong River from its mouth at Phillipsburg on the Delaware to its source at Lake Hopatcong, then following the sharp descent of the Passaic River to its mouth at the Hudson, almost directly opposite Manhattan. Neither stream was navigable, but by a remarkable feat of engineering, such a canal was built: the Morris Canal, which opened for business in 1831, before railroads had begun to show how quickly the canal would be superceded by the iron highway as the primary transportation mode. The Morris Canal also served the important iron-mining region of Morris County, in the mid-19th century before the opening of the Missabe Range in Minnesota one of the three most important iron-mining areas of the nation. The Morris Canal connected with the Lehigh Canal at Phillipsburg for the movement of coal and other commodities across the state.

As seemed to be the case everywhere, railroads began to challenge canals almost as soon as they were built in the East. The Morris Canal's days were numbered as soon as the Morris & Essex Railroad began to move from east to west across the state. The M&E built west from Newark. In 1865, it achieved its goal of bridging the northern part of New Jersey and reached the Delaware at Phillipsburg. It could now load coal from the Lehigh Canal boats, but by then it was apparent that the future lay in all-rail routings of coal. The obvious partner for the M&E was the Delaware, Lackawanna & Western, which moved coal down from the Northern Anthracite Region around the Lackawanna and Susquehanna rivers through the Delaware Water Gap, then into New Jersey over its subsidiary, the Warren Railroad, to connect with the Central Railroad of New Jersey at Hampton. Acquisition of the M&E, which connected with the Warren Railroad at Washington, New Jersey, would give the Lackawanna its own route into the New York area. In 1868, the DL&W, cash-rich from the lucrative anthracite trade, acquired the Morris & Essex and absorbed it into its growing system.

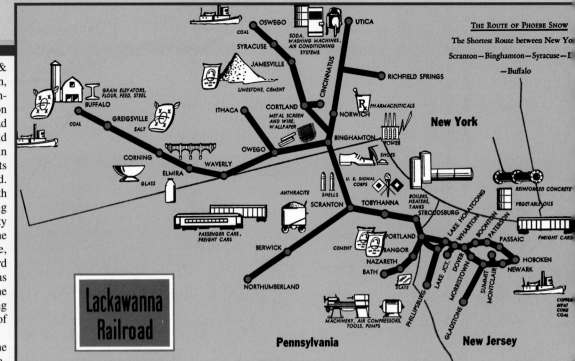

The Delaware, Lackawanna & Western had its origins at Scranton, in the Lackawanna Valley of northeastern Pennsylvania. The Scranton brothers, George and Selden, had started an iron works along the wild lands of the Lackawanna Valley in the 1840s, and had secured contracts to build rail for the Erie Railroad. The Scrantons built railroads north and east from their burgeoning industrial empire at the community named for them, and combined the two roads into the Delaware, Lackawanna & Western. The hard coal of the Lackawanna Valley was fueling not just the foundries of the Scranton's iron industry, but flowing in great quantity to the consumers of the Northeast as well.

The Morris & Essex was not the only railroad to be built in northwestern New Jersey. The Sussex Railroad was built between 1851 and 1866 to serve the largely agricultural region of Sussex County. It connected with the canal and the M&E at Waterloo. It was a minor factor in its own right, but a potential competing link between the upper Delaware Valley and connections to New York. The Lackawanna acquired it in 1881 to prevent the threat of such competition, and the 21.5-mile line settled into the role of a local carrier of milk, commuters from the far suburban fringe of Greater New York, and freight for the farms and stores of Sussex County.

As the Lackawanna became a major player in New Jersey rail activities, it began to show that it was not afraid to spend money on its rail facilities. Over the years, this became a dominant theme of Lackawanna corporate management: build the finest lines and facilities, buy the best equipment, and maintain the track and engines and buildings to the highest standards. In the years of King Coal, the money was there to do this, and the Lackawanna emerged as a first-class railroad in every respect.

In the eastern part of its evolving New Jersey rail empire, an opportunity for a major improvement presented itself with the construction of a second major line between Denville, in Morris County, and Hoboken by way of Boonton and Paterson. This route had been chartered in the 1840s but never built, and the M&E acquired the rights to the line at roughly the same time as the Lackawanna takeover. With the Lackawanna's abundant capital behind it, the new line was built quickly, opening in 1870, dropping down from Denville above the Rockaway Valley through Paterson and Passaic to the Jersey Meadows and a connection with the M&E at the Bergen Tunnel. The original M&E line through the Oranges and Summit to Morristown and Dover had been built more with an eye to connecting major communities than for its railroad logic: it had to climb the Watchung Hills with an almost frontal assault that gave it a tough grade of over 1.5% to Summit. It also passed through the densely populated zone of the Oranges and Newark. The Boonton Line allowed the road to route its freight to waterside on a gentler grade, out of the way of most of the passenger operations on the original M&E, and became the conveyor belt of anthracite and, after the Lackawanna reached Buffalo in 1883, of freight from the Midwest and West that reached New York over the beautifully built right of way of the DL&W in New York and Pennsylvania.

The greatest years of the Lackawanna were the years when the hard coal trade – the mining, movement, and sale of the commodity – was dominated by a monopoly put together by banker J. P. Morgan in the 1890s. Most of the coal that was mined came from lands and mines owned by the big anthracite railroads, and competition among them was limited by their sense of shared interest and an equal dislike for the vagaries of the free market. The Big Five anthracite carriers were the Reading, Lehigh Valley, Lackawanna, Delaware & Hudson, and Jersey Central, with the New York, Ontario & Western, Erie and Pennsylvania also significant participants in the hard coal industry. Morgan was able to direct the fortunes of the entire

rail industry in the 1890s and early years of the new century, with the effect of reducing the risks that buccaneer capitalism had created in earlier years. The Lackawanna fell under the control of the Vanderbilts, even though its superb and direct New York to Buffalo line was a major competitor of the Vanderbilt's princely New York Central. But in those years, there was plenty of business for all, and no thought of combining systems that were, in effect, working in concert already. The Lackawanna concentrated on improving its physical plant and its rolling stock and engines, all of which by the second decade of the 20th century were second to none. The profits rolled in, the future looked bright, and the hardest thing for the road's managers was to find good ways to spend all their riches.

The most visible result of this period of affluence was the enormous investment in the railroad right-of-way, which produced the lasting image of the Lackawanna: huge fills and cuts, a razor-sharp ballast edge on fine double track main lines, huge bridges of concrete arch design spanning entire valleys, well-built towers and stations along the lines, few road crossings at grade. It was a super-railroad in every way but one: size. In the cartel arrangement of the Morgan approach, expansion by merger or acquisition was out, and the railroads cooperated with one another. When government regulation replaced the informal private-sector arrangements, the result was much the same. The rich Lackawanna remained the compact and regional railroad it was to stay, confined to a New York to Buffalo route it had to share with four other major roads.

The first years of the 20th century saw the final development of the Lackawanna system in New Jersey. A second bore was added to the Bergen Tunnel, which was built in 1877 for a direct entrance to New York Harbor at Hoboken. The southern part of the Sussex Branch assumed great importance as the Lackawanna partnered with the Lehigh & Hudson River for a share of the traffic between Buffalo and New England over the New Haven's Maybrook Line. Trains operated between Port Morris on the Lackawanna and Maybrook by using the Sussex Branch to the L&HR at Andover Junction, then the L&HR to the great interchange yard at Maybrook. Efficient operation of the service made it competitive with that of the Erie, which connected directly with the New Haven at Maybrook, and was a major source of traffic for the railroad right up to the formation of Erie-Lackawanna.

By far the most dramatic improvement of the period was the construction of the Lackawanna Cutoff between Port Morris and the Delaware Water Gap, opened to traffic in 1911. A look at the map shows the wisdom of this massive project. The old east/west mainline crossed the river south of the Water Gap and headed in a southeasterly direction to Washington, where it switched to a northeasterly path through Port Morris to the east. It was the result of the Lackawanna piecing together its route from existing railroads. With abundant money available, and the latest construction methods able to conquer the hills and valleys of northwest New Jersey, the great Cutoff eliminated the loop of the Old Main through Washington in favor of a straight, double-track path from Port Morris to the Delaware. It saved 11 miles in distance, a major factor in the competitive New York-Buffalo trade, and was built to the highest possible standards. Two major concrete arch bridges, over Paulin's Kill at Hainesburg and the Delaware River, were required, and these set the railroad world on its head with their massive and beautiful design. Complementing the Cutoff in New Jersey was a similar project between Clarks Summit and Hallstead, Pennsylvania. The old main line was replaced with a straighter and less heavily graded right of way that saved only four miles of distance, but increased the speed and efficiency of operations west of Scranton. The highlight of this stretch was the huge concrete arch bridge over Tunkhannock Creek that dwarfed the Paulin's Kill span and was the largest bridge of its type ever built when opened in 1915. The Lackawanna could rightly claim to be the leader in railroad engineering and right-of-way construction by the second decade of the century.

The Lackawanna reaped the benefits of its investments through the 1920s, as demand for anthracite as a home-heating fuel stayed high, and the road got its share of the freight and passenger business between New York, New England, and Buffalo. Large on-line communities like Scranton and Binghamton provided significant business as well. As commuters flocked to the pleasant towns and rural areas of its northern New Jersey territory, the Lackawanna invested in the late 1920s in electrification of its major commuter line on the former M&E, including the branches to Gladstone and Montclair.

In the locomotive department, the Lackawanna also broke ground. It had always stabled exquisite locomotives, but by the 1920s its Pacifics and Mikados were too small to handle the increased train sizes efficiently and speedily. Three-cylinder Mountains were successfully added to the locomotive fleet in the 1920s, but the railroad made a wise decision in 1927 by settling on the 4-8-4 wheel arrangement for both freight and passenger locomotion. Eschewing the common name of "Northern" for its new engines, it called them "Poconos" after the mountains of eastern Pennsylvania that provided them with their stiffest challenge. The Lackawanna became the first user of the 4-8-4 type in the East, and over time acquired 55 Poconos in four orders, in 1927, 1929, 1932, and 1934. More than any other steam engine, the Pocono type became synonymous with the Lackawanna in the final years of steam. The steam locomotive fleet reached its final form in 1937 with the arrival of five gorgeous, high-drivered Hudson types for fast passenger service. Many consider these 4-6-4s among the most handsome steam engines ever built.

World War II put an enormous strain on the Lackawanna, as it did with railroads nationwide. Anthracite coal shipments reached and even exceeded the levels of the 1920s, after a disastrous drop in the 1930s. New York Harbor saw a constant stream of troop ships and freighters heading to Europe, with the Lackawanna providing its share of the business. By the end of the war, the Lackawanna looked to the diesel-electric locomotive to replace its steam locomotives. With characteristic willingness to spend its earnings on improvements, and with the Poconos showing their age and hard years of service, the railroad dieselized quickly, beginning with EMD's pioneer FT type in 1945. Between 1945 and 1953, when the final steam operations took place, the Lackawanna seemed to sample almost every type of EMD cab unit, settling on F units as its major type for freight service and a fleet of 11 E8As for its long-distance passenger operations, after a brief flirtation with steam-heater equipped F3s for its varnish. It added diesel switchers from Alco and EMD (with a few GE units thrown in), and road-switchers from EMD, Alco and Fairbanks-Morse after its last order of F7s in 1949. In 1953, as steam was finally leaving the stage and again in 1956, it ordered its last new diesel road units from Fairbanks-Morse, the brutish Train Master, the only road-switchers delivered in the handsome maroon and gray paint scheme. The diesel fleet received the usual high level of Lackawanna maintenance, and was virtually intact at the time of the E-L merger in October 1960.

Along with dieselization came an upgrade in the line's premier passenger train. The LACKAWANNA LIMITED was a nice New York/Buffalo train with a mundane name and standard equipment. In 1949, Lackawanna president William White decided to create a new image for the train, ordering matched streamlined equipment in the maroon and gray colors of the diesels, and renaming it PHOEBE SNOW to recreate the famous theme of the early days of the century, when anthracite was extolled as a clean fuel that a mademoiselle like Miss Phoebe could ride behind without soiling her pure white clothing. Even though the road was phasing out steam, and anthracite was a dying industry, the image worked, and no one questioned the logic of the name change. It was a breathtakingly beautiful train, with equipment and amenities that put it among the finest trains in the East.

The new diesels and the PHOEBE SNOW helped to hide the situation the Lackawanna found itself in as the 1950s deepened. It was no longer a major force in the industry, as shown by the rebuffing it received from the Nickel Plate, its major Buffalo connection, to suggestions of a Lackawanna-led merger in 1952. The Delaware & Hudson was also approached, and declined as well, seeing no great advantage to a merger with either the Lackawanna or Nickel Plate. Anthracite was in a steep decline that by decade's end made it virtually a dead industry. The St. Lawrence Seaway cut into the traditional business done at the Buffalo gateway, and made it imperative to have a bridge route to the Chicago area. Like every Eastern road, the Lackawanna feared the consequences of a merger between the two regional giants, the New York Central and the Pennsylvania, and saw merger as the only ameliorative to the desperate situation it was in. Lacking options, the road settled on a marriage between itself and its neighbor, the Erie. In the past, few nearby roads seemed so different in their fortunes than the rich and self-absorbed Lackawanna and the perennially bankrupt and weak Erie. But the merger seemed to make some sense, and the roads began to consolidate some aspects of their operations even before the October 17, 1960 formal merger. The Erie moved into the Lackawanna's Hoboken Terminal in 1956. In 1959, the Lackawanna began routing its trains over the parallel Erie trackage between Binghamton and Corning, providing savings as the redundant trackage was ripped up or reduced to local service.

Merger brought with it further reductions in the Lackawanna's once world-class right-of-way. Much of the Buffalo Division trackage was removed in favor of a route west of Corning via the Erie lines through Hornell, and much of the former Buffalo bridge traffic stayed on E-L tracks heading for the Midwest. The PHOEBE SNOW became a minor Buffalo connection for the merged road's premier New York/Chicago train, which reverted to the banal approach to naming of the past as the ERIE-LACKAWANNA LIMITED. The Maybrook routing via Port Morris was now also redundant, and the New England traffic moved along the former Erie directly to Maybrook.

Just as the Lackawanna heritage seem to be passing from the scene, the failing E-L turned to a former Lackawanna president, the highly respected and experienced William S. White, for salvation. White had left the Lackawanna in 1952 for the presidency of the New York Central, but lost that job when Robert Young gained control of the Central and installed Alfred Perlman as president. White moved quickly to the Delaware & Hudson's top job, and had the satisfaction of seeing the D&H prosper while the Lackawanna and Central's fortune declined through merger and financial woes. White brought some needed life back into the ailing Erie-Lackawanna, which under his leadership dropped the hyphen and became the *Erie Lackawanna*. After years of mismanagement by the Erie team, and the adoption of a somber black and yellow Erie-derived color scheme, the EL under White seemed like a return to the Lackawanna, with a color scheme identical to the beautiful scheme introduced in the 1940s, and the ERIE LACKAWANNA LIMITED renamed PHOEBE SNOW (even though it followed the Erie tracks west of Binghamton to Chicago instead of Lackawanna rails to Buffalo). In New Jersey, though, it used the Lackawanna from Hoboken over the M&E and Cutoff to Pennsylvania and points west, so the renaming brought back the glory of the Lackawanna on its home rails in the Garden State.

In the end, the Lackawanna lost out because it was just too small in an era of railroading that saw the growth of mega-railroads through merger and acquisition. But right to the end, to the merger with the Erie in October of 1960, it was fair to say that the Lackawanna packed a variety of lines and operations that made the region it served seem much larger than in fact it was. Let's review its operations and setting by a westward trip on the Lackawanna, starting at the banks of the Hudson at Hoboken.

New York Harbor

Above ■ Let's begin our trip on the Lackawanna the way that untold thousands of travelers did, crossing the blue water of the Hudson River from Lower Manhattan to the ferry terminal at Hoboken. The Lackawanna's ferry service was operated by its subsidiary, the Hoboken Ferry Company. We're on the deck of one of the ferries approaching the Hoboken Terminal on April 4, 1957, about to enter one of the six slips that served the Lackawanna. We've certainly begun our trip at Barclay Street Terminal in Manhattan, because at this date the other two locations that the Lackawanna ferries once served, at 23rd Street and Christopher Street, were no longer in use. The ferry *Lackawanna* docked at the right of the picture was the oddball of the fleet, as indicated by its much lower stack. It was re-engined with a diesel prime mover in 1949; the rest of the fleet was steam powered. Dieselization even intruded on the railroad's ferry operations in the 1940s! Note also the large "Erie" lettering above the name Lackawanna. This is still in the pre-merger period, but the Erie moved its commuter operations from its Jersey Central rail and ferry terminal to the Lackawanna's much larger and more accommodating Hoboken Terminal prior to the merger, in 1957. *(Ted Gay/H. Peterson collection)*

Above ■ The Lackawanna's ferries were painted an attractive shade of light brown with shaded gold lettering beginning in the early 1940s. Prior to their repainting they wore white, with gold lettering. Color shots of the ferries in white are very rare, so we are fortunate to be able to start this volume with a shot of the *Binghamton* heading across the Hudson from New Jersey to Manhattan around 1940. The vessels were veterans of decades of service on the cross-Hudson operation, having been built in the first decade of the 20th century.

(Charles E. Nagle/Mark Schmidt collection)

Above ▪ Few sights in the world were as dramatic as the Manhattan skyline. With the deep waters of New York Harbor indigo in the twilight, two of the Lackawanna ferries are visible going about their time-honored business of carrying commuters and patrons of the Lackawanna's intercity trains between Gotham and Hoboken. The Barclay Street ferry terminal is blocked by the wharf to the right; it is almost directly beneath the "World Telegram" letters on the building at the right center of the picture. By the time this shot was taken in February 1963, the E-L diamond has replaced the square Lackawanna emblem on the high smokestacks of the ferries, but otherwise the scene is one that greeted decades of riders in Lackawanna days. The service ended on November 22, 1967, forcing commuters to choose either bus or PATH service to reach their jobs in Manhattan. *(Ted Gay/H. Peterson collection)*

Above ▪ The Lackawanna conveyed freight cars as well as passengers and vehicles across the Hudson to New York City. Pier 13 was close to the Barclay Street ferry terminal in lower Manhattan. Wearing a weathered shade of green, it presented this appearance on a sunny, brisk winter day, February 22, 1953.
(Mike Del Vecchio collection)

Harlem Transfer

Above ▪ The diesel era in American railroad history began with little fanfare and no indication of the transformation it would bring to the railroad scene. Among the first targets of opportunity for the diesel were the switching operations around New York's harborside trackage. The Kaufman Act, enacted by the state of New York in 1923, forbade the use of steam power in New York City beginning in 1926. The ban on steam helped to lift the stage on internal combustion engines, which seemed the answer for railroads operating isolated terminals around New York Harbor. This group included the Erie, CNJ, Baltimore & Ohio, and Lehigh Valley as well as the Lackawanna. The box-cab diesel-electrics produced by the consortium of American Locomotive/General Electric/Ingersoll-Rand were the state of the art in diesel design in 1926, when the Harlem Transfer Company, a Lackawanna subsidiary, received its #2, painted in standard locomotive black with gold lettering. There was no #1 on the Harlem Transfer; the 2 was part of a two-unit order by the Lackawanna, which assigned the number the 3001 to the first unit, lettered for the Lackawanna, and 2 for the Harlem Transfer instead of Lackawanna 3002 as originally planned. The unit worked at the Bronx location operated by the Harlem Transfer, one of three Lackawanna terminals in New York that were served by carfloats from Hoboken. The other two were in South Brooklyn, which received the 3001, and at Wallabout Bay in Williamsburg, Brooklyn, which used overhead electric wires to power a steeple-cab GE electric motor numbered 4001 instead of a diesel. Harlem Transfer 2 was a long-lived unit, serving for over 35 years at the company's Bronx terminal. It is pictured here in the last year of service, working at Pier 36 in the Bronx, transferring hopper cars from the car float. *(Matthew Herson)*

Right ▪ Miraculously, the builder's plate was still on the ancient boxcab diesel in 1961. Screwed securely to the cracked and crazed black paint, the 2's heritage is laid out on its metal birth certificate, noting the consortium of three builders that put their expertise together to begin the diesel revolution. Curiously, the plate gives builder's numbers for GE and Alco but not Ingersoll-Rand, the company that is usually associated with these early boxcabs. *(Matthew Herson)*

Above ▪ The bright January sun shows off the lines, if you can call them that, of the 2 at its Bronx bailiwick beginning its last full year of service. At one time, New York City had many of these almost hidden little pockets of rail activity, controlled little environments that provided safe havens for archaic engines like the 2 that would long ago have been traded in if they had been in regular service. *(Matthew Herson)*

Hoboken Passenger Terminal

Above ▪ In the early 1950s around 35,000 commuters a day passed through the Lackawanna's Hoboken Terminal. Some rode in on electric-powered trains from Dover on the Morris & Essex and the Gladstone and Montclair branches. Others came by way of the Boonton Line from as far west as Branchville and Washington. Most continued to their jobs in the financial district of lower Manhattan on one of the nine ferries operated by the Hoboken Ferry Company, a Lackawanna-owned company. The terminal dated back to 1907, and had 17 platforms to accommodate the commuter rush and the still-considerable number of intercity trains of the Lackawanna. The New Jersey side of the Hudson opposite Manhattan had an array of passenger terminals then. The CNJ, Reading, and Baltimore & Ohio terminated at the CNJ's Jersey City Terminal. The Erie also terminated at Jersey City, while the New York Central's West Shore line and its tenant, the New York, Ontario & Western terminated just to the north of Hoboken at Weehawken. Only the Pennsylvania and its affiliated road, the Lehigh Valley, penetrated the barrier of the Hudson to drop their patrons off directly in Manhattan. On March 14, 1953 a short local from Montclair is coming into Hoboken Terminal, passing Hoboken Tower. *(Henry W. Peterson)*

Above ▪ A steam-powered train from the Boonton Line has dropped off its passengers at the terminal, and its Pacific is backing the train back to the coach yard to wait for the evening rush hour and the return trip to the suburbs. The 1119 is part of the fleet of 4-6-2s that was the backbone of the steam commuter service in the last years of steam operation out of Hoboken. It's one of the high-drivered ones, with 79" driving wheels that originally were assigned to the crack passenger trains of the Lackawanna, one of five built by Alco in 1922. The Railway Express Building in the background was a landmark at Hoboken, and a good prop for pictures with its billboard lettering. *(Frank Watson)*

Above ▪ On February 13, 1949, the westbound LACKAWANNA LIMITED was lined up to head west from Hoboken. In 1949, the only passenger diesels on the Lackawanna were the passenger F3s, like the 801 set doing the honors this day. The F units still have gray roofs, soon to be painted black to hide better the grime from the exhaust of the engines. In November of 1949, the new PHOEBE SNOW will be christened, and the name LACKAWANNA LIMITED will be consigned to history.
(Arthur Angstadt/Hawk Mountain Chapter NRHS collection)

Right ▪ George M. Leilich, Vice-President of Operations for the Western Maryland, was also an excellent rail photographer. He was at the Hoboken Terminal in July 1957 and made this moody shot of E8 810 inside the dimly lit trainshed, a difficult spot to take pictures. *(George M. Leilich)*

Below ▪ The late Robert F. Collins captured the look of the Hoboken Terminal on a snowy February 17, 1958, the low afternoon light barely illuminating the MU cars ready to take the commuters back to their homes in the New Jersey suburbs. By the time their day is over, it will be dark, as it will when they pick up their morning train to return to work. The terminal had 18 tracks. In 1956 the Erie began routing its passenger trains to Hoboken in one of the first cooperative ventures between the Erie and the Lackawanna. At the time, the two roads operated 446 daily trains into Hoboken (292 on the Lackawanna, 154 on the Erie) with around 85,000 passengers served daily. This was, by any standards, a busy place. *(Robert F. Collins)*

Above ▪ Lackawanna train #5, the TWILIGHT LIMITED, is in position to load passengers for its run to in 1959. The TWILIGHT was a popular train to Buffalo, with through cars for Detroit and Chicago. Its 4:50 departure time from Hoboken was a prime time for most travelers leaving the New York area for an overnight run to the Midwest, or to return to on-line cities after a full day in Gotham. *(Joseph McCarthy)*

Left ▪ On August 1, 1959, noted railroad photographer Arthur Angstadt of Allentown, Pennsylvania and his friend Kenneth Von Steuben were at Hoboken to ride the Lackawanna. They were not the only out of town visitors at Hoboken that day. For a brief period, the Lackawanna was using its Fairbanks-Morse freight units on passenger trains. The 930 was one of six H-16-44s that the Lackawanna bought from Fairbanks-Morse in late 1952. The H-16s were most often found working local freights around Port Morris and Bangor, Pennsylvania. We'll see more of Mr. Angstadt's coverage of the Lackawanna later in this volume, in his home state of Pennsylvania.
(Arthur Angstadt /
Hawk Mountain Chapter NRHS collection)

On July 11, 1960 train #1067 to Washington was about to depart Hoboken behind F3 802C for the 61-mile run out to the hills of Warren County. *(Al Holtz)*

Above ▪ Although most people think of Hoboken as the Lackawanna's Hudson River terminus, the riverside freight yard was right at the boundary between the cities of Hoboken and Jersey City, with most of the facility in Jersey City. In February 1958, Joseph McCarthy took these remarkable pictures from the grain dock. Looking to the northeast, the coal dock is in operation, although the Lackawanna doesn't seem well represented in the loaded coal hoppers on the pier. The Empire State Building rises through the haze of Manhattan in the distance. *(Joseph McCarthy)*

Below ▪ Looking now to the southeast, the docks for car floats are visible. The Lackawanna operated car float service to several locations in New York harbor. *(Joseph McCarthy)*

Jersey City Freight Facilities

Above ▪ The view to the southwest shows the considerable size of the Lackawanna's freight yard at Hoboken/Jersey City. In the background, Bergen Hill is visible, the natural barrier the Lackawanna had to tunnel through to reach tidewater. *(Joseph McCarthy)*

Pages 14/15 ▪ The final view is to the northwest. The coal yard is off to the right, and we get a good view of the grain unloading facility itself.

(Joseph McCarthy)

In 1953-54 the Lackawanna touted its New York Harbor capabilities in its advertising.

Hoboken Engine Terminal

Above ▪ Pacific 1135 was under steam at Hoboken on April 3, 1953. The 1135 was one of the most powerful of the Lackawanna Pacifics, the group numbered 1131-1135, which developed just under 50,000 pounds of tractive effort, more than enough for the moderate sized commuter trains they operated at the end of steam. These engines had relatively low drivers of 73" and were built by Alco in 1915. The steam locomotives assigned to the Boonton Line trains to Dover, Washington, and the Sussex Branch congregated around Hoboken in the mid-day hours, coming in from the west in the morning inbound rush and returning in the evening. There were some trains spaced throughout the day, but there was always something tempting to shoot around the engine terminal. On weekends the service was thinner, and more engines were present. The darker time of year is better for mid-day shooting, before the sun gets too high, and shots tend to look shadowy. Steam locomotives were tough to shoot in color, with all but the lowest light conditions leading to some shadowing, as in this case with the 1135. The 1135 was one of the Pacifics fitted with a snowplow pilot, and has the full ladder steps leading from the pilot to the running boards. *(E. P. Griffith)*

Above ▪ The 1121 was also at Hoboken on April 3, 1953 as steam operations wound down to their final weeks. The 1121 was a high-drivered thoroughbred that powered the Lackawanna's best trains west of Scranton until the Hudsons arrived in 1937 to take over those duties. The 1121 was equipped with 79" drivers, and was built in 1920. In just two months and two days from the day Ed Griffith shot it in Hoboken, the 1121 would close the steam era on the Lackawanna, hauling train #1067 west on June 5. After that, the snazzy Pacific with the aluminum-painted smokebox and stainless steel lettering did stints as a stationary boiler at several locations, not meeting the wrecker's torch until 1955. It shows some differences in its front end details from the 1135, with only a single step to assist crewmen climbing from the pilot to the running boards. *(E. P. Griffith)*

F Units

Right ▪ When the first FTs arrived on the Lackawanna in 1945, they started a program of dieselizing the railroad's freight operations with EMD cab units, ending with the purchase of F7s in 1949. In addition to the bulk of the F unit fleet bought for freight service, the Lackawanna also began dieselizing its passenger trains with F3s until it decided upon the E8 as its passenger engine of choice. More than any other type of diesel, the F unit came to symbolize the Lackawanna in the diesel era. Part of the allure was the two different color schemes used by the railroad for its cab units, one for the freight units and another for the passenger engines. Both utilized the same colors, gray/maroon/yellow, in more or less the same manner, with a yellow nose and maroon striping and lettering on a base of gray, and each had the unmistakable look of EMD designers, with curves and stripes that fit the contours of the F unit body in a graceful and elegant manner. EMD and Lackawanna produced a pair of classics, colors and designs that made an immediate and lasting impact on anyone who saw them, unlike any other road's diesels. The 621 set, an A/B/A F3 locomotive, posed at the La Grange, Illinois plant for the EMD photographer in January 1948. The 621 was a low-geared F3 bought for pusher service, but looks much too classy for such mundane work. Note some of the details that will change as the 621 settles in to work on the Lackawanna: it will get a continuation of the upper stripe connecting the two side portholes on the A units, a red headlight will be installed on the nose door, and black paint will cover the roofs of the units. *(Electro Motive Division)*

Right, Center ▪ The Lackawanna was a thing of the past and the Erie-Lackawanna was in its third month of operation when Joseph McCarthy photographed the 660A. The Lackawanna's numbering system for its F units was rather confusing. Locomotives were ordered as A/B/A, A/A, or A/B sets, with a three-digit number covering all units in a particular locomotive and the suffix A, B, or C for the individual units. No four-unit orders were made, so no units bore the suffix D; all booster units were B's. This numbering approach was used by many railroads that considered multiple-unit sets of Fs as single locomotives. What compounded the confusion was that Lackawanna numbered the Fs in two separate categories. Road units began with the 601 FT set and a second number series began with the 651 and continued up through 662. The higher-numbered units were for lower speed service and helper duty. Confusion was heaped upon confusion by the lack of continuity in the number series. The FT sets were numbered 601-4 and the first F3 sets continued the sequence, numbered 605-606. The next F3s broke the sequence by being numbered 621 A/B/C. These were low-speed units also, the only A/B/C set ordered for drag service. When the F7s came in 1949, the first set was the 611A/B/C, then the sequence shifted to 631 and continued on to 636. All the F7s but the 631 came as A/B locomotives. The 631 was ordered as an A/C set, so there was no 631B but there was a 631C, the only F7 with a C for a suffix. The higher numbers were for lower-geared units delivered for helper service. The engines in the 650-series were all delivered as A/B sets, hence there was no need to include the A suffix in the number board, as there was in the 600-series engines that included both A and C designated cab units. No F7s were delivered as lower-geared engines. The Lackawanna also ordered five A/B/A sets of F3s equipped with steam boilers for passenger service, numbered 801-805 A/B/C. Got all that?

(Joseph McCarthy)

Above ▪ A fine shot of the Hoboken engine terminal by Joe McCarthy shows the 654 A/B set at JC Pit in October 1957, hooked up with Phase II Train Master 851 and F7A 636, the newest F unit on the roster. The 654 A/B was one of the four A/B sets of FTs purchased for helper service out of Scranton. By the 1950s, the Lackawanna had come to the realization that overspecialization of diesel assignments was inefficient, and mixed and matched its diesels as required. *(Joseph McCarthy)*

Above ▪ The 804A illustrates the look of the passenger F3s, delivered to the road in 1947 in the passenger scheme that became the standard for the road in the 1950s. The 804A has the two portholes and low fans of a Phase III F3, differentiating it from the other A unit in the consist, one of the Phase I F3s with three side portholes and high fans. Notice also that Lackawanna B units bore no road name. The corrugated steel building in the background is the Lackawanna electric equipment inspection and repair shop. *(Joseph McCarthy)*

Above ▪ A handsome A/A set of passenger F3s sits beside the electric shop at Hoboken in June 1958. These engines had been built to power the premier passenger runs, but after delivery of the E8s were bumped to more mundane assignments, on Boonton and Washington locals. Two A units were often used, to avoid wying of the power for the return trip. Note that the passenger F3s did not have the reflectorized number boards below the headlights that the Lackawanna employed on its freight cab units. *(Joseph McCarthy)*

Above ▪ The 802A and C show off the Phase I design, with three portholes on the side. These units dated all the way back to December 1946. This nicely lit shot highlights two of the unusual touches on the Lackawanna Fs, the visor over the upper headlight and the yellow paint around the portholes. Both have plagued Lackawanna modelers for years! The units were photographed between runs at Hoboken in December 1960, but have yet to be renumbered for new owner Erie-Lackawanna. *(Joseph McCarthy)*

Right ▪ The first of the Lackawanna's freight F3s were Phase I units. The 605A shows off the freight scheme on this style of F unit car body at Hoboken in June 1959. The 605A was involved in a wreck in 1959 and was scrapped, never making it into the E-L roster.
(Joseph McCarthy)

Left ▪ Hoboken's Henderson Street Terminal is an F unit paradise in June 1959. Even a healthy coat of grime and the typical Jersey haze can't totally dull the sharp appearance of the four Lackawanna F unit sets in town. From the left, we see F3 658, F3 804-C, F7 631-A, and F7 632. *(J. J. Wheelihan)*

Above ▪ F7 636 heads west out of Hoboken in October 1957 with the skyscrapers of Manhattan forming an impressive background. Like many of the big railroads in the New York/New Jersey area, the Lackawanna brought mainline freights right down to the water's edge, facilitating carfloat service to various locations around New York Harbor. The train has a block of piggyback trailers on the head end. The Lackawanna was an early entrant into the intermodal trade, beginning piggyback service in 1954. Its major partner in the Buffalo gateway, the Nickel Plate, was also getting into the business in 1954 and working together the two lines inaugurated service from New York west to several Midwestern cities. The trailers were conveyed on 40-feet flatcars built at the Keyser Valley Shops in Scranton from obsolete hopper cars. The trailers were 32' in length. *(Joseph McCarthy)*

Left ▪ After the Erie moved its commuter operations from its Jersey City terminal to the Lackawanna's Hoboken facility, Erie diesels began laying-over at Hoboken between runs. Unlike the Lackawanna, the Erie favored road switchers for its commuter trains, and had no electrified lines. Several Alco units and a GP7 shared the Hoboken scene with a Lackawanna F3 in the fall of 1959. *(J. J. Wheelihan)*

Above ▪ By 1952, the dieselization of the Lackawanna was in its final stages. Steam was holding out mostly on the local passenger trains in New Jersey. Trains on the Boonton Line, the Old Line, and the Sussex Branch were still rolling into Hoboken with Pacifics and Hudsons on the head end. Although the Lackawanna was heavily invested in EMD cab units, Fs and Es, they were not well suited for local passenger service, especially on light trains where a single unit might suffice. Cab units had to be turned at the end of such runs, unlike road switchers. Many of the other railroads around the New York area that had similar non-electrified commuter service turned to the Alco RS3. But the RS3, with only 1,600 horsepower, was a bit underpowered for some of the Lackawanna's purposes. A better answer seemed to be a new and perhaps revolutionary product from Fairbanks-Morse, the big and burly Train Master. The Train Master, at 2,400 horsepower, was in some ways the first "second generation" unit, a diesel that was designed not just to best steam but to correct the deficiencies of the first round of diesels that had replaced them. Although FM was one of the minority builders, without the track record of reliability of EMD, the Train Master seemed to be a perfect fit for the Lackawanna. The Lackawanna had bought its first engines from Fairbanks-Morse in 1952, a group of six H-16-44 road switchers, so turning to the builder for additional power was not something that happened out of the blue. The Train Master

was the drag racer of the diesel era, not just high-horsepower but the quickest diesel to accelerate from a standing stop. For locals with lots of stops, this was a real plus. The other thing touted by the folks from Beloit was the ability of the Train Master to haul mainline freight as well, with that speed advantage of importance here, too, for the Lackawanna in their highly competitive New York/Buffalo run. The Lackawanna decided on the Train Master as the engine that met their needs. While many other roads continued to buy cab units into the early 1950s, the Lackawanna bought ten of the huge Train Masters in 1953. As passenger units, they got the passenger paint scheme, adapted from the gentle curves of the EMD bulldog nose to the immense and angular bulk of the FM design. The result was another triumph of aesthetics. Few road switchers looked as impressive as the second of the ten units delivered in the summer of 1953, the 851, which posed for the photographer in September of that year in the company of an ancient wood boxcar. (*Edward Miller collection*)

Above ▪ The original Lackawanna Train Master, the 850, was shot by the Fairbanks-Morse photographer outside the factory in Beloit, Wisconsin.

(*Fairbanks-Morse Corporation*)

Above ▪ The 858 was hooked up to the 850 at Hoboken in February 1958. The 858 shows off the look of the short hood on the Phase I units, with the headlight mounted lower than on the newer Train Masters the Lackawanna bought in 1956. *(Joseph McCarthy)*

Below ▪ The Lackawanna went back to FM for two additional Train Masters in 1956. The local passenger service was already dieselized – and in decline – so the 860 and 861 were purchased exclusively for freight service. Nonetheless, they got the passenger paint scheme the same as the other ten. By this time, the design of the Train Master had changed somewhat. The 860 posed with the 859, one of the first ten of the type, at Hoboken in April 1959. *(Joseph McCarthy)*

Switchers and Road Switchers

Right ▪ Lackawanna EMD end-cab switcher 560 was shunting refrigerator cars at Hoboken in 1959. It was one of ten SW9s on the railroad, built between 1951 and 1953; the 560 was the newest of the group, built in June 1953 as the Lackawanna was retiring the last of its steam switchers. The big yellow road lettering added needed color to the solid black switchers, whose small size accentuated the bold lettering. *(Joseph McCarthy)*

Above ▪ The Lackawanna acquired 20 GP7s from EMD between 1951 and 1953. The units were used in local freight and passenger service primarily, but occasionally were added to mainline freight consists (and rarer yet, as boosters on mainline passenger runs). They had the legendary GP7 dependability, and gave good service to the railroad. Even though they were expected to hold down passenger assignments on the Washington and Sussex Branch trains, they were painted in the solid black scheme used by the railroad for its switchers and roadswitchers. Lacking any decoration besides the imitation gold lettering and road number, they were very plain machines. The 970, the highest-numbered of the group, was at Hoboken engine terminal in February 1958. *(Joseph McCarthy)*

Left ▪ The Lackawanna bought six H16-44s from Fairbanks-Morse in 1952. Outside its Beloit birthplace the 933 stood for its formal portrait.

(Fairbanks-Morse)

Above ▪ The westbound PHOEBE SNOW is kicking up the snow near Harrison. The photographer's notes indicate that the usually dependable #3 was running three hours late on this snowy day in February 1958. The train has an unusual combination of engines, two F3s leading a lone E8, suggesting that the delay may have been caused by a breakdown on another E8, since the Es always traveled in pairs on the PHOEBE. Whatever the explanation, it's a marvelous panorama of the Jersey Meadows, taken from the parallel tracks of the Pennsylvania, with the state's largest city, Newark, in the distance. *(Joseph McCarthy)*

Morris & Essex

Above ▪ The Lackawanna's main predecessor line in New Jersey was the Morris & Essex. The name persisted as the name for one of the Lackawanna's three operating divisions (Morris & Essex, Scranton, and Buffalo). The M&E Division encompassed all lines east of Stroudsburg, including the Bangor & Portland Branch in Pennsylvania and all the trackage in New Jersey. Our tour will begin with the oldest sections of the railroad, heading west from Hoboken over the electrified line through Newark and Morristown to its connection with the Boonton Line at Denville, after which we will retrace our trip west over the Boonton Line and continue west.

A westbound commuter train is heading out the M&E through the Jersey Meadows at Kearney in 1949. It's a classic scene of New Jersey railroading captured by perhaps the greatest rail photographer from a state that has produced more than its share of railfans: Robert F. Collins, who often ventured over from his job at the DL&W's fiercest rival, the Erie, to shoot the steam engines of the Lackawanna and occasionally also its electric and diesel power. Three pantographs up mean this is a six-car train; the Lackawanna ran its MU cars as tractor/trailer pairs. The lead car is one of the ten combines built in 1925, before the electrification project was begun, and converted to MU control trailers in 1930. The jointed rail and the ballast edge are razor straight, as befitting a railroad that cared greatly about top-flight maintenance of its physical plant. *(Robert F. Collins)*

The Oranges

Above ▪ An eastbound Scoot catches the light near Brick Church station on December 13, 1958. *(Richard Solomon)*

Left ▪ Young Joe McCarthy stood a safe distance from the hulking black mass of Pocono 1505 waiting at Brick Church station in East Orange to take the LACKAWANNA LIMITED west on September 23, 1943. The 1505 was one of the five original Poconos, the 1501-1505, which arrived on the railroad in 1927. They were the first 4-8-4s in the Northeast, and began the modernization of the Lackawanna's mainline steam fleet that ultimately numbered 55 Poconos and five Hudsons. The 1500s were considered to be expendable when the first passenger diesels arrived on the scene in 1946/47, and the 1505 was apparently the last of the five to see service, as a pusher assigned out of Port Morris.

(Joseph McCarthy collection)

Above ▪ The late morning departure time of the PHOEBE SNOW from Hoboken made shots of the head end power overly backlit, but it meant that the gorgeous tavern/lounge/observation car proudly bearing the train name was set up perfectly for well lit shots. Train #3 is heading west from Brick Church Station in February 1960.

(Joseph McCarthy)

Above ▪ The last light of December 13, 1952 catches a westbound extra steaming through East Orange. This may be an extra carrying the overflow mail from the Christmas rush, at a time when most mail still moved over the rails, and 3 cents was all you needed for a first-class letter. *(Henry W. Peterson)*

Gladstone and Montclair Branches

Above ▪ The usual two-set, four-car train is at Stirling Station, 8.6 miles west of Summit on the Gladstone Branch. This roughly 21-mile branch left the M&E main at West Summit and headed southwest through a pleasant, almost rural suburban region of small towns and wealthy homeowners who wanted a distinctly rural environment within easy reach of Newark and New York. The Gladstone Branch originally bore the grandiose and misleading name of the Passaic and Delaware Railroad. Although it never came close to the latter river, although the name "P&D" stuck, and was used long after the line was part of the Lackawanna. It was acquired by the Lackawanna in 1882 through lease, and reached its final length by extending to Gladstone in 1890. The first electrics began operating on January 6, 1931, and the line became a favorite one for railfans to shoot the MU trains. This shot is undated, but by the looks of the Studebaker parked by the station, it's probably the middle 1950s. *(Ted Gay/H. Peterson collection)*

Above ▪ A Nor'easter of mammoth proportions pounded New Jersey in March 1956, dropping heavy snow that threatened to cripple the Lackawanna's electrified lines. At Millington on March 19th, a four-car train is already covered with the white stuff as more falls, adding to the miseries of commuters but nothing compared to the problems of those relying on the snow-covered roads. The few patrons with cars left at the Millington station will have some digging to do. Millington is 10 miles west of Summit, roughly the halfway point on the branch.

(Henry W. Peterson)

Above ▪ The Gladstone Branch seemed like the quintessential commuter line, but it also generated a healthy freight business from a rock quarry at Millington. Two RS3s have a rock train in tow at Millington. The Lackawanna had no electric freight power, unless you count the short-lived "three-power" units that could operate on battery, oil engine, or overhead electric power. These engines were used exclusively in the Secaucus/Hoboken/Jersey City terminal area. Steam and then diesel locomotives provided the motive power for the P&D freight operations. *(Bill Hopping)*

Left ▪ The west end of track on the P&D was at Gladstone, shown here in May 1959. There was nothing special there, just a nice suburban station and tracks to store the trains at night waiting for the morning rush. Hoboken was 42.26 miles to the east. *(Richard Solomon)*

Morristown

Right ▪ Morristown, known as a community of millionaires in the days around the turn of the 20th century, is the seat of Morris County. The Morris & Essex reached Morristown the first day of 1838, three years after it was chartered. Morristown was a shade less than 30 miles from Hoboken and a stop for the intercity trains as well as Scoots. Eastbound #6, the PHOEBE SNOW, is rolling into the station at Morristown with both the 816's headlights shining in this nicely backlit image from Dr. C. K. Botkin in July 1952. *(Dr. C. K. Botkin)*

Below ▪ After the PHOEBE SNOW headed east, eastbound deadhead X92 appeared with Pacific 1119 heading toward Hoboken past the station, visible to the right of the picture. The 1119 gained renown as the only Lackawanna steam engine converted to burn oil instead of coal. *(Dr. C. K. Botkin)*

Morristown & Erie

Above ▪ The M&E connected with a pair of short-lines, the Rahway Valley at Summit and the Morristown & Erie at Morristown. The latter operated an enginehouse at Morristown, and ran 10.5 miles up the Whippany River valley to Essex Fells, connecting there with the Caldwell Branch of the Erie. Posing in the high sun on the turntable at Essex Fells in mid-1952 is Alco switcher 14, bearing the name *Mauritius Jensen* on the cab, and the crewmen. The red paint scheme looks attractive on the engine, a brand-new S4, and bears the slogan of the road, "Service is our business." *(Henry G. Becker)*

Above ▪ At the Morristown roundhouse, two Morristown & Erie 2-8-0s, the 10 and the 12, get some attention in September 1955. *(Henry G. Becker)*

Above ▪ Morris Plains, 32 miles west of Hoboken, featured a nice brick station with a tiled roof. The PHOEBE SNOW rolled past the station westbound on November 7, 1958.

(Ted Gay/H. Peterson collection)

 Western Morris County

Right ▪ Eastbound train #26 from Scranton was a good passenger train to shoot in morning light, leaving Scranton at daybreak and getting into Hoboken at 9:35 Eastern Standard Time. Early in November 1957 the train passed Tabor Lake as it neared Morris Plains with E8 812 handling the train solo, the norm for the MERCHANTS LIMITED.

(Bill Hopping)

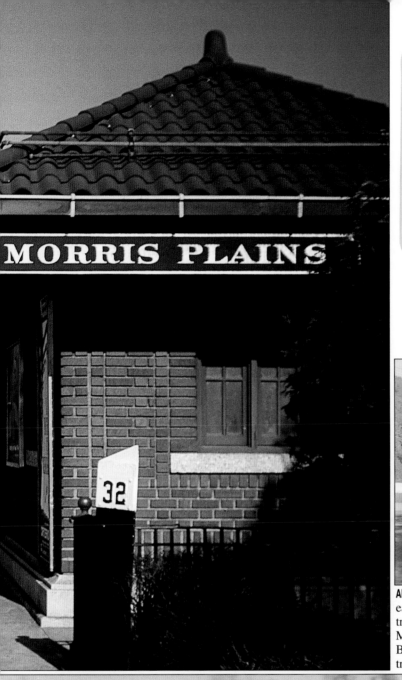

MORRIS PLAINS

32

William White's facsimile signature appeared on the 1948-49 Lackawanna pass. He would return over a decade later to resuscitate the flagging Erie-Lackawanna.

Above ▪ The MERCHANTS LIMITED passed the station at Mt. Tabor on its eastbound morning run from Scranton in the fall of 1957. Through trains like #26 didn't stop at Mount Tabor; the nearest stop was Morristown. We'll head back to Hoboken for the trip west over the Boonton Line before returning to Denville for the remainder of our trip west to the Delaware River. *(Bill Hopping)*

The M&E route west from Hoboken had the advantage of serving the heavily populated Newark metropolitan area, but it was less than satisfactory as a route for the heavy coal traffic that began to move from Pennsylvania to the Hudson River after the DL&W assumed control in the 1860s. The M&E suffered from problems that could be traced back to its origins; it was built at a time when railroads served a limited, local market, and could not meet demands that were unimaginable in the early years of the railroad industry. The answer lay in a second route from central New Jersey to Hoboken that was designed to minimize grades, curves, and densely populated urban corridors. The Boonton Line was begun in 1868, the year the DL&W took charge of the M&E, and finished in 1870. It descended the hills of Morris County to Paterson and Passaic, rejoining the M&E at West End Tower, at the west side of Bergen Hill. There was no

way to avoid the climb from sea level at Hoboken to the heights of hilly Morris County, where the Lackawanna attained an elevation of 970 feet above sea level, but the Boonton Line served its purpose well. It was approximately 34 miles from Hoboken to the junction with the original M&E main line at Denville. The Boonton Line carried all the through freight trains on the Lackawanna, a few through passenger and express trains, and local passenger trains between Hoboken and the Old Road and the Sussex Branch. The line was not electrified, so it took on a very different character from the M&E. As steam disappeared from the Lackawanna, the Boonton Line was a bastion of steam right up to the end in 1953, making it the favored location for rail photographers who preferred steam over electric MU's. We will examine this busy artery from east to west, beginning with Secaucus Yard in the Jersey Meadows.

Above ▪ Secaucus Yard in the Jersey Meadows was not a location that most Lackawanna fans flocked to see. Spreading across the meadows west of Bergen Hill, 3.7 miles west of Hoboken on the Boonton Line, it was not especially scenic nor especially welcoming to fans. Heading into Secaucus is this bizarre combination of esoteric equipment, one of the General Electric/Ingersoll-Rand center-cab units acquired by the Lackawanna in 1933/34 leading a Boonton Line open-vestibule combine on what appears to be a dead-head move. It was one of six of the 102-ton GE/IR units acquired as part of the drive to dieselize switching operations around the Hudson. The GE/IR units were commonly seen around Hoboken Terminal, which is where this move originated.

(Don Ball collection)

Above ▪ In the late fall of 1960 three Train Masters move an eastbound freight out of Secaucus Yard toward the end of track at Henderson Street in Hoboken. The units are still showing their three-digit Lackawanna numbers, which will acquire an extra digit "1" after the merger. *(Joseph McCarthy)*

Above ▪ The dual-service Train Masters became fixtures on the Boonton Line trains after the end of steam in 1953. Four years into its tour of duty on the Lackawanna, the 858 looks clean as new, leading a short westbound local into the station at Passaic, 10.57 miles west of Hoboken, in July 1957. Although FM engines were generally a flop, high on maintenance costs and low on reliability, the Train Master was probably the company's best product. The Lackawanna got a lot of miles out of their 12 units, in both freight and passenger service. But given the declining financial condition of the road in the late 1950s, wholesale replacement of locomotives was not a viable option.

(Al Holtz)

Above ▪ Heading east through Clifton on the morning of May 31, 1951 was Hudson 1151, the first of the six high-drivered 4-6-4s the Lackawanna acquired in 1937 for its top passenger trains. Bumped by the F3s from those assignments, the speedy engines found a second life, hauling commuters on the Washington to Hoboken run. Looking a great deal like a shorter version of the handsome Poconos delivered in 1934, the 1150s had 80" drivers and were similar in many respects to another, more famous Alco-built Hudson, the New York Central's J-3 4-6-4. The 1151 left Washington at 6:25 in the morning, and will return (as we will see on pages 36, 40 and 43) on #1053 in the evening, after servicing at Hoboken. Bob Collins knew about the Hudsons on the Washington trains, and went over to the Lackawanna expressly to catch them in this rare service. It's certain he wasn't disappointed. *(Robert F. Collins)*

Right, Center ▪ Laying down a good smoke plume, Pacific 1137 headed east through Clifton with train #1020 on May 31, 1951. The hills in the background announce that the terrain west of here becomes increasingly rugged as we move from the flatlands around the Jersey Meadows to the rolling country of north-central New Jersey.
(Robert F. Collins)

Right ▪ Westbound trains through Clifton enjoyed a nice stretch of straight tangent track before starting to curve up through the hills around Paterson. This was one of Bob Collins' favorite places to find Lackawanna steam in action. The area was open enough to allow a good deal of light to illuminate the scene. The signal bridge provided a nice prop also, seen here spanning the three tracks as westbound #1053 heads for Washington on July 29, 1952 behind Pacific 1133. Some of the more adventuresome commuters are enjoying the natural air conditioning provided by the fine New Jersey air, with a bit of coal smoke added from the exhaust of the 4-6-2. *(Robert F. Collins)*

Above ▪ There is nothing to compare with the sweet low light of a summer evening to bring out the essence of a scene. The low light angle was especially important to capture the detail of a steam engine in color. Summer was over and turning to fall when shot Pacific 1116 bringing westbound train 1055 under the signal bridge at Clifton on September 29, 1952. The 4-6-2 is laying down a perfect plume of smoke that certainly pleased the photographer, but would have been anathema to Miss Phoebe Snow and her dress of white. There would be no more Septembers for the 1116 and the other remaining steam engines on the Lackawanna roster. The last steam commuter run was on June 5, 1953. *(Robert F. Collins)*

Above ▪ Earlier on the evening of July 29, 1952, train #1049 headed west a bit to the west of the shot of the #1053 with the 1125 putting on a nice display of dark smoke for photographer Collins. *(Robert F. Collins)*

Above ▪ Northern New Jersey still had some room to grow in the early 1950s, as suburban sprawl moved west from the New York area to the hills of Passaic and Morris counties. The green field in the background at Clifton seems incongruous this close to Hoboken. Snowplow-equipped Pacific 1135 is really pouring it on heading west to Washington with train #1053 on May 20, 1953, two weeks before diesels will douse the fires of steam on the Boonton Line trains. Lackawanna frowned on excessive smoke, so we can assume it was for the benefit of the photographer. *(Robert F. Collins)*

Right ▪ Racing west through the Clifton tangent was Hudson 1151 on its usual assignment in the summer of 1951, train #1053, a long-distance local bound for Washington. The Hudsons were the epitome of elegance, with aluminum painted smokebox, stainless steel raised lettering and numbers, but were also extremely capable, with tractive effort of over 52,000 pounds that made them among the most powerful of their type ever built. *(Robert F. Collins)*

Right ▪ Mr. Collins didn't get his usual perfect smoke plume from the fireman of Pacific 1140 leading train #1055 west through Clifton on August 23, 1951. *(Robert F. Collins)*

Paterson

Above ▪ Robert F. Collins was not the only master photographer to leave us with a record of Lackawanna steam in color on the Boonton Line. Ed Griffith was out shooting at Paterson in the last year of steam operation, and left us with memorable images like this of Pacific 1135 dropping down the grade below the Paterson station with good-sized eastbound train #1016 from Washington, New Jersey on April 20, 1953. *(E. P. Griffith)*

Left ▪ The imposing heights above the Paterson station are snowless and barren on January 17, 1953 but lit nicely by the bright early morning light as Pacific 1137 accelerates out of the station with eastbound train #1110. Is there any better combination of elements for a railroad picture than blue sky, morning light, and white steam from a hard-working locomotive? *(E. P. Griffith)*

From a vantage point high atop Garrett Mountain, photographer Richard Solomon captured this remarkable scene of an eastbound Lackawanna freight passing the Paterson station and entering the built-up industrial region of Paterson/Passaic. Aside from Newark, Paterson was the largest city in New Jersey served by the Lackawanna. As the location of the station shows, the Lackawanna was more interested in through traffic on the Boonton Line than serving the communities along the way. The Lackawanna station was on the edge of the city, while the Erie, whose tracks are visible in the background, went right through

West Paterson

Above ▪ The rugged terrain around West Paterson provided an intrepid rail photographer like Bob Collins some great hike-in locations to shoot the westbound commuter rush, still in steam in the early 1950s. The six 4-6-4s that joined the Lackawanna roster in 1937 were the newest and arguably the handsomest engines on the DL&W roster. Designed for fast running on the long tangents of the Buffalo Division, they were only ten years old when the passenger F3s replaced steam on the top passenger assignments. Like a Hall of Fame ballplayer asked to pinch hit at the twilight of his career, Hudson 1151 is hauling a lowly commuter train, #1053, west to Washington at West Paterson on May 31, 1951, hard on the heels of #1049. Usually the longest of the afternoon trains, #1053 was scheduled out of Hoboken at 5:30 in the afternoon, and ran with as many as 10 coaches, so it was the usual train to find the Hudsons on in 1951, along with counterpart morning eastbound train #1016. *(Robert F. Collins)*

Right ▪ The next spring Bob was back at West Paterson for the great show of Lackawanna steam on the Boonton Line trains. The 1118 was heading west with a four-car train on April 21, 1952. The trees have not yet begun to leaf out, and the shadows still stretch over the tracks in places, but another year of shooting the evening trains has begun on the Boonton Line. The star of the show, Hudson 1151, was gone, though – the Hudsons were all retired by 1952, with the 1152 the last to see service. The final two years of steam operation on the Boonton trains was entrusted to the fleet of Pacifics.

(Robert F. Collins)

Above ▪ One of the most spectacular locations on the Boonton Line was the Paterson High Bridge over the Passaic River at West Paterson. The 70-feet tall trestle provided a nice open location for trains in the days before I-80 eliminated this portion of the Boonton Line. The suburban revolution was moving out to the hills west of Paterson, as shown by the new single-family homes under construction on the hillside in the background. For a view of this bridge in diesel days, see the excellent shot of a Train Master at almost this identical location in Morning Sun's *Lackawanna Railroad in Color (Volume 1)* taken by Al Holtz in 1957. By then, the houses were occupied, and steam was gone from the Lackawanna. Bob Collins got there in the last week of steam operation on trains like this one, #1053, crossing the bridge on the evening of June 2, 1953 with the 1137 for power. Only three days later, the last steam passenger trains will leave Hoboken for the trip over the Boonton Line. *(Robert F. Collins)*

Right ▪ On New Year's Day of 1953 Ed Griffith was at Totowa as a westbound steams by with Pacific 1125. *(E. P. Griffith)*

Mountain View

Above ▪ Winter was a great time of year to photograph steam locomotives in action, the cold air turning the exhaust steam white from contact. Pacific 1123 was trailing a beautiful white plume at Mountain View on December 19, 1952 with train #1051. *(Robert F. Collins)*

Right ▪ Down at track level at Mountain View, Robert Collins shot train #1031 behind the 1120 on January 12, 1952. The red number board below the headlight was a nice touch of color on the Lackawanna steam engines; not all had them, and early color photographs like this are invaluable guides to modelers to show detail items like this.

(Robert F. Collins)

Left — The high hills of western New Jersey form a nice background for an eastbound train from the Sussex Branch passing Mountain View on the morning of June 19, 1952. One of the ubiquitous Pacifics, this one with a black-painted front numberboard, is powering the little train east toward Hoboken.

(Robert F. Collins)

Left, Center — Hudson 1151 led westbound train #1053 through Mountain View on July 3, 1951, no doubt having little trouble with the good-sized local. One has to respect early color photographers like Bob Collins, who ventured out in the 1940s and early 1950s with slow Kodachrome film to record the parade of westbound trains leaving Hoboken in the evening rush, knowing that they would be barely able to freeze trains like this in the dwindling light.

(Robert F. Collins)

Below — Mountain View Tower a half-mile west of the station at Mountain View controlled the crossing of the Boonton Line and the Erie's Greenwood Lake Branch. Eastbound freight NE-4 is bearing down on the crossing with F3 633 as the leader of a four-unit set, which gives a clue that this undated shot is sometime close to the end of the Lackawanna, when four-unit lashups were increasingly common. In the 1960s, Mountain View assumed great importance as the Boonton Line through Paterson was severed and a new connection was built at Mountain View so that I-80 could utilize the Boonton Line right-of-way to the east. *(Jack Emerick /*
W. T. Greenberg collection)

Boonton

Above ▪ Boonton, 29 miles west of Hoboken, was situated above the Rockaway Gorge. In the mid-1800s it shared in the iron industry that dominated the economy of western Morris County, and remained a source of traffic for the Lackawanna in later years. On September 30, 1961, an A/B/B/A set of FTs entered Boonton with an empty sand train. It's E-L now, and the FTs will start to disappear from the new road's roster as soon as it can get together the cash to invest in newer power. *(W. T. Greenberg)*

Above ▪ A pair of F3s is in charge of train #1059 at the Boonton station on October 1, 1961. Two Borden's milk cars trail the diesels, a very rare commodity to still see on the rails in the 1960s, and are heading west to the Sussex Branch for loading.

(W. T. Greenberg)

Left ▪ It's a year plus a month and two days into the E-L era as westbound freight HB-9 moves through Boonton behind a trio of Train Masters renumbered for the new road on November 19, 1961. Things haven't yet changed too much, and HB-9 is still one of the top freights on the Lackawanna rails. Starting at Hoboken, it made the run over the Boonton Line to Port Morris, where it picked up New England traffic brought down from Maybrook by the Lehigh & Hudson River's train #31 scheduled to arrive at Port Morris just before noon.

(W. T. Greenberg)

Denville

Below ▪ Denville was the point at which the two lines from Hoboken, the Boonton Line and the Morris & Essex, joined, making it a favorite spot for train-watchers who could catch the action on both the Lackawanna mainlines. The Denville depot stood at the point where the two lines converged. The M&E catenary continued west to Dover, the end of the line for the electrification. On August 2, 1952 the 1116 is coasting into the station at Denville on its eastbound run to Hoboken, with a single rider waiting to catch the train. *(Ted Gay/H. Peterson collection)*

Above ▪ A westbound freight on the Boonton Line passes through Denville as a drill waits in the clear on the lead from the old line through Rockaway. Photographer Dick Townley is getting a serious look from the fireman on F7 634, lead unit of the locomotive consist that includes also an F3B, and F7B, and an RS3 as the trailing unit. *(Dick Townley)*

Above ▪ A pair of Train Masters heads east on the Boonton Line, passing the Denville station and the M&E heading off to the left. This overhead angle captures the massive look of the rectangular FMs. If you look carefully at the first unit, you can see that the Lackawanna took great care to ensure that the color scheme on the Train Masters matched that of the passenger cab units, making sure the striping and the pointed end of the lower yellow stripe were the same height along the step-up of the running board at the end of the long hood. Painting and decaling models of the Lackawanna Train Masters have always been a challenge, but just as it was on the real railroad, the effect is magical. *(Bill Hopping)*

Above ▪ A ridge just east of the Denville station afforded photographer Bill Hopping a good angle to shoot RS3 906 with a cut of empty hoppers. The engineer appears to be looking back over the hoppers, perhaps in anticipation of a backup move. Empty hoppers were not uncommon, though, on the M&E, heading back to the quarry at Millington on the P&D. *(Bill Hopping)*

Right ▪ In April of 1950 an eastbound local powered by a Pacific was approaching the station at Denville, at the point where the Boonton Line separates from the M&E.

(Steven Hepler collection)

Right, Center ▪ Following the passenger train east on the Boonton Line that day in April 1950 was a freight led by one of the remaining Poconos. By the beginning of 1950, the fleet of Poconos had been trimmed from a high of 55 by the scrapping of the original five, the 1501-1505, and the Lackawanna would continue to retire the Poconos by seniority on the roster until the end of steam operations in 1953. This appears to be one of the 1620s built in 1932, with spoked 70" drivers and a center-mounted headlight.

(Steven Hepler collection)

Below ▪ On a beautiful summer morning in 1950 Steve Bogen caught Mikado 1256 on the eastbound Boonton Drill at Denville. The 1256 was one of the lighter Mikados, built by Alco in 1920. This train left Port Morris Yard in the morning and switched various customers at Denville and Boonton. It always had a cut of tank cars for the E. F. Drew Company in Boonton, a big source of traffic for the Lackawanna. Steam under the wires always made an interesting subject for photography.

(Steve Bogen)

Above ▪ The Young coal yard bagged the blue coal into 50-pound bags for retail sales. Lawyer S. Young, Senior shows the years of hard work required to keep this type of business going, weighing the bags on a movable scale in January 1960. *(William S. Young)*

Rockaway Loop

Above ▪ When the Morris & Essex extended its line west from Dover, they routed the line to the north to serve the important iron-mining region around the town of Rockaway. The line was retained after the construction of the Boonton Line on a more direct route between Dover and Denville. After passenger service to Rockaway ended in 1948, the loop served local industries such as L. S. Young & Sons Coal in Denville. Anthracite was historically a home heating fuel, and hundreds of small coal yards like this were the heart and soul of the industry when it provided heat to households across the Northeast. Two of the company's International trucks pose proudly in August 1954 by the sign that says it all: "Blue Coal: Steady Heat, Real Comfort." Judging from the four-digit number on the truck door, Denville has not yet enjoyed the convenience of dial telephones.

(William S. Young)

Above ▪ Here's how the blue coal was unloaded from the hoppers for bagging. A CNJ car was being unloaded at L. S. Young & Sons in January 1960. *(William S. Young)*

Above ▪ Fortunately for us, one of the sons in the Lawyer S. Young & Sons enterprise was William S. Young, a railfan and photographer, who provided us with these images of the family business and many other fine shots of the Lackawanna in action. Bill Young posed by the company's dump truck at the Denville coal yard.
(Steven Hepler collection)

Right ▪ The loop from Denville through Rockaway was used to provide passenger service to Rockaway until a final run was made on October 17, 1948. Paul Reynolds was among the many local residents and railfans who turned out at the Rockaway station for the poignant occasion. *(Paul Reynolds)*

Above ▪ For a few days in May 1955, a strange-looking train was spotted on the loop track in Denville. American Car & Foundry's Talgo Train was there to be filmed for a promotional piece on the virtues of light-weight trains, built to a Spanish design and finished off in an orange and aluminum color scheme. The cars were built at ACF's Berwick, Pennsylvania plant on the Lackawanna's Bloomsburg Branch. The Lackawanna was apparently just a convenient location for the filming, since it provided little in the way of a potential sale for a lightweight train like this midget. *(William S. Young)*

Dover

Above ▪ The Lackawanna followed the Rockaway River's path into Dover. The westbound PHOEBE SNOW was cruising into Dover on November 20, 1960, a month into the new Erie-Lackawanna era. Heading west, the hills get higher and higher, and the far hills are faintly visible in the distance. The Rockaway River's blue waters are off to the right of the tracks in this fine panorama taken from the Franklin Road bridge. The area to the left was once the location of the East Dover car shops.

(M. Del Vecchio collection)

Above ▪ Dover was the center of the iron-making industry of Morris County, and was called the "Pittsburgh of New Jersey", certainly an overstatement, but nonetheless reflective of the former importance of iron in the development of western New Jersey. Dover's large brick station, built in 1903, dominated the railroad scene at this important point on the Lackawanna, a stop for through and commuter trains and terminus for some local runs. *(Richard Solomon)*

Right ▪ Dover Tower was across the tracks from the station. It was a wooden structure of standard DL&W design and color. A derailment on August 20, 1952 allowed the manual "Armstrong" switches to be replaced by electronically operated turnouts, although the Armstrong levers were retained to serve the new system. The tower lasted past the merger and into the 1980s before being closed in 1984 and torn down in 1989. Operator Russell Ruff is on duty at the tower, with the model board and levers on the right of the shot. *(William S. Young)*

Right, Center ▪ The eastbound Pocono Express paused at the Dover station in late spring 1951 with two sparkling new E8s, the 814/813 for power. The Pocono Express, train #2, was due into Dover at 1:45 PM, having left Buffalo at 4:25 AM with through cars from Detroit and Chicago. *(Paul Reynolds)*

Below ▪ The engineer is looking back from his perch in the cab of the 814 for the signal to leave the Dover station to finish its run to Hoboken. The early afternoon sun favors the shot facing east, accentuating the long lines of the E units being admired by the young gentleman to the right of the picture. The Nickel Plate RPO car has come through from Chicago, and is an indication of the close relationship of the two roads, which at this point in history are still considering the merger that is not to be, one that could have led to a dramatically different future for the Lackawanna and the whole railroad map of the East. Even after the merger plans fell through, the Lackawanna retained its valuable Nickel Plate stock until impending bankruptcy forced management to sell it off in 1959 to help pay the mounting bills. *(Paul Reynolds)*

Above ■ The light catches the lead unit of train #3, the westbound PHOEBE SNOW, as it makes its scheduled station stop at Dover on October 7, 1960. The PHOEBE was scheduled out of Hoboken at 10:35 AM, and made the run up the M&E to Dover in under an hour, arriving around 11:15. The morning schedule made the train somewhat hard to photograph, with the light generally opposing, so we are indebted to photographer Ted Gay for his skill in composing the shot to allow the slight backlighting to highlight the colors of the beautiful streamliner, just ten days before the merger.

(Ted Gay/H. Peterson collection)

Above ■ What a difference a day makes! The sun is shining on March 20, 1956 and Dover is digging out from the blizzard that blanketed the state the day before. The sun will soon melt the snow on the roof of the depot, and it will be business as usual in the Garden State. *(William S. Young)*

West of the Wires

Above ▪ West of the end of catenary, E8 816 crossed the Rockaway River heading into Dover with #6, the eastbound PHOEBE SNOW, at 5:30 PM on a Sunday afternoon in the late 1950s. The eastbound PHOEBE SNOW was scheduled for a daylight run in each direction. Leaving Buffalo at 10:15, it was scheduled through Scranton at 3:15 PM and into Hoboken at 6:30 in the evening. A nice way to spend a day! *(Al Holtz)*

Below ▪ Al Holtz found a good spot to shoot eastbound trains at Waterworks Park on the west side of Dover. Train Master 859 led a train from the Sussex Branch east in the spring of 1957.
(Al Holtz)

Above ▪ The eastbound PHOEBE SNOW also rolled into Dover behind E8 818. Composing the shot properly with so many elements – the train, the pole line, the winding dirt lane, and the shadows – took skill and imagination. It worked; all the factors combined for a memorable shot of a great train. *(Al Holtz)*

Lake Hopatcong

Left ▪ Lake Hopatcong is the biggest natural lake in New Jersey, and sits at New Jersey's equivalent of the continental divide, with waters to the east flowing to the Hudson and to the west to the Delaware. This was the highest elevation the Lackawanna reached in the state. The Lake Hopatcong station was a magnificent affair, with a castle-like stone headhouse and a massive concrete pedestrian crossing; it was built between 1910 and 1911. A westbound freight led by an A/B/B/A FT set is heading under the walkway in the summer of 1958. The station headhouse is on the hillside to the right of the tracks.

(J. J. Wheelihan)

Above ▪ On Thursday, August 11, 1960, the ground around the station is shaking as westbound HB-9 passes with an A/B/B/A set of FTs. By this time train size dictated four-unit sets of FTs, and this set contains the 601C leading the 603B and the other two units in the 601 set, the B and A. The train is hauling 93 cars into Port Morris Yard, a few miles ahead, where it will pick up cars brought down from the New Haven by the Lehigh & Hudson River's train #31. *(J. J. Wheelihan)*

Above ▪ On August 18, 1957 Lake Hopatcong is the scene of a meet between the westbound PHOEBE SNOW and an eastbound freight with a set of F units for power. *(Ted Gay/H. Peterson collection)*

Above ▪ E8 819 is blurred as it speeds train #26, the eastbound MERCHANTS LIMITED from Scranton past the stopped westbound HB-7 at Lake Hopatcong at 8:37 in the morning of July 2, 1957. Train #26 was usually the only intercity train of the Lackawanna to show up with a single E8. It was a daily-except-Sunday run, and was the best way for Scrantonians to spend a day in New York. If returning the same day, they could head back on train #11, the SCRANTONIAN, or wait for train #5, the TWILIGHT LIMITED, which left an hour later. *(Bill Hopping)*

Port Morris

Above – Port Morris, 46.5 miles west of Hoboken, was a strategically located hub of operations in western New Jersey. Situated at the highest point on the railroad in the state, it was the eastern end of the Lackawanna Cutoff, and close to the end of the Sussex Branch, with its important bridge traffic to the New Haven at Maybrook in conjunction with the Lehigh & Hudson River. In Lackawanna days it was the scene of constant action, with through trains setting off and adding cars, and trains dispatched to the cement district and various New Jersey locations to serve local industries. Steam switcher 210 was shunting loaded hoppers at Port Morris in February 1950. Behind the 0-8-0 is Port Morris Junction Tower, identified by the letters UN, which controlled movements at this busy location. The 210 was one of the 60 0-8-0s built at the road's shops at Scranton using the boilers from older Mikados and Pacifics between 1929 and 1935. The result was a modern and powerful steam switcher, and the road continued to employ these engines long after its program of dieselization for road power had begun. The 210 was one of the engines rebuilt from the freight Pacifics.

(Dick Townley)

Above – The Lackawanna acquired a total of 18 RS3s between 1950 and 1952, using them mostly in local freight service. Unlike some of its neighboring roads, it did not use them in commuter service (like the Erie, the CNJ and the Reading) or in solid lashups for road service (like the L&HR and D&H). The black RS3s were seen usually as single units or in pairs on roustabout freights. Port Morris was a good place to find the RS3s, which were dispatched in several directions on a daily basis on local freights. Bill Hopping got the whole five-man crew to pose with the 914 at Port Morris. The RS3 has the characteristic aluminum-painted horn and stack of RS3s assigned to Port Morris. *(Bill Hopping)*

Netcong

Above ▪ The station at Netcong served both the Sussex Branch and the Old Road trains from opposite sides of the depot. In February 1953 4-6-2 1119 has a short train on the Sussex Branch side of the station heading east to Hoboken.

(Robert F. Collins)

Below ▪ On August 31, 1957 GP7 968 led a short eastbound train off the Sussex Branch at the Netcong passenger station. Five of the 20 GP7s, numbers 966 through 970, were equipped to handle passenger trains, and the light trains of the Sussex Branch were suited to the 1,500 horsepower units. Looking at the stark black carbody makes one wonder why the Lackawanna, normally so image-conscious, didn't at least come up with a yellow version of the square emblem it applied to the cab units.

(Arthur Angstadt/Hawk Mountain Chapter NRHS collection)

Usually if a photographer fails to lead the train fully into the picture the result is a disaster. But when the foreground is something as interesting – dare we say "funky" – as the station at Cranberry Lake, we thank the photographer, in this case Bill Ellis, for his foresight in allowing the structure and not the train to dominate the scene. Cranberry Lake was the first stop up the branch from Netcong, five miles away. *(William Ellis)*

Right ▪ We're looking back over a train stopping to pick up passengers at the Cranberry Lake station on a beautiful October day. The wooden milk car on the front of the train is a reminder of how important the milk business was for the Sussex Branch, which passed through a lightly populated, largely rural area still outside the suburban sprawl that is now engulfing Sussex County. *(Mike Del Vecchio collection)*

Below ▪ Heading west (compass north) from Cranberry Lake the branch dropped down the 2.7% grade to Andover and crossed the Lehigh & Hudson River main line at grade at Andover Junction. In a scene that captures the small-town feel of the Sussex Branch, Train Master 852 passed the station at Andover with an eastbound train. This is not the urban, industrial New Jersey that lays only a short train ride to the east. The Lackawanna used the dual-service FM units just as their builder had promoted them, and they became the usual power, along with the passenger GP7s, on the Sussex trains in the 1950s. *(Bill Hopping)*

Above ▪ Its stop completed, the train heads for Netcong through the wooded town. *(Bill Hopping)*

Below ▪ Wooden caboose 767 brings up the rear of a westbound freight train at Andover. Unlike neighboring roads Reading, CNJ, L&HR, and Lehigh Valley, the Lackawanna did not acquire the steel "Northeastern" caboose, relying on wood cars 600-849 until the arrival of steel cabooses rebuilt from the tenders of scrapped steam engines. *(Bill Hopping)*

Above – The Lackawanna shared in the important bridge traffic between the Midwest and New England by partnering with the Lehigh & Hudson River Railway, in which it shared ownership with the L&HR's other connecting railroads. The Sussex Branch connected with the L&HR at Andover Junction, and the New England trains were run to and from Port Morris Yard over this stretch of track. The cars received from the L&HR were then quickly blocked onto westbound freights for the run to Buffalo. L&HR crews and engines were stationed at Port Morris for the run up to Maybrook and back, with at least two round trips run daily. Port Morris is at a higher elevation than Andover Junction, requiring the westbound trains to climb a 2.7% grade once they left the L&HR and headed over the branch. Helpers were needed, and the system was to run a Lackawanna engine from Port Morris, attach to the L&HR road engine and doublehead up the grade to Netcong and into the yard. In 1941, William McChesney recorded this scene of a Lackawanna 4-6-2 helping one of the Lehigh & Hudson River's huge 2-8-0s on a westbound train that just passed through the tunnel under the Lackawanna Cutoff at Andover. *(William McChesney)*

Above – After dieselization, the Port Morris/Maybrook trains were entrusted to Alco RS3s. The L&HR dieselized entirely with the 1,600 horsepower units, buying 13 of them, and it was common to find a Lackawanna RS3 head light from Port Morris to Andover Junction to help the L&HR units up the grade to the yard. The 915 is near the Route 206 crossing at Andover Junction waiting for the Maybrook train to arrive on the L&HR for the final lap of the trip to Port Morris, where the cars will be quickly put on a freight bound for Buffalo. *(Bill Hopping)*

Above ▪ Newton, 60 miles from Hoboken and eight miles up the branch from Netcong, was the seat of Sussex County, settled originally in the 1760s. Newton possessed a fine county courthouse built in 1847 and a fine set of railroad buildings, including a large two-story station with train-order board and a water tank. There was a small yard with a turntable behind the station for trains laying over at night awaiting the morning return to Hoboken. Robert Collins found 4-6-2 1116 at Newton on March 13, 1949. The first two trains eastbound on the branch in the morning left from Newton while later trains left from the end of the branch at Branchville. Notice how the water tank is set up to rewater the engines on the main track and not the yard tracks. *(Robert F. Collins)*

Left ▪ Train Master 854 headed west from Newton for Branchville with a good-sized train. *(Bill Hopping)*

Above ▪ At Straders, 2.75 miles from the end of track at Branchville, two GP7s are backing down the lead to Henry Becker's Creamery. *(Bill Hopping)*

Above ▪ Branchville was the end of the line, and was served by a substantial wooden station wearing a weathered coat of Lackawanna green paint. The Sussex Branch might have continued westward as part of a through line, but the Lackawanna feared it might become a competing route east for Pennsylvania coal, and purchased it in 1881 to preclude any such development. It was notable for the number of rail lines it crossed in its modest 21.5 mile length, crossing under the Lackawanna Cutoff at Andover and crossing at grade the L&HR, Susquehanna, and L&NE. *(Mike Del Vecchio collection)*

Above & Below ■ In the summer of 1946, peace returned to the United States, and the railroads were planning their postwar strategies. Over 90% of the nation's freight and passenger loadings had moved over the rails during the war, and 1946 continued the great demand for rail services. It would take some time for the supply of new cars to meet the public's demands, for new roads and airports to take the business away from the railroads. For affluent roads like the Lackawanna, the big decisions had to do with motive power and new rolling stock. The success of the FTs made it only a matter of time before diesels cut more and more into the steam roster. For fans of steam, 1946 was a great year to be out shooting photos again, without the strain of wartime restrictions on film and gasoline, and without the vigilance necessitated by the need for national security. For fans of steam, it was the time to be trackside, the first hours of the long twilight that for the Lackawanna would end with total dieselization in 1953. In that hopeful summer of 1946, big-boilered 2-8-2 2141 was working on the Old Road at the Hackettstown freight house. The 2141 was one of the 10 modern Mikados built for the Lackawanna in the mid-1920s. These were the largest of their type on the railroad, and among the biggest Mikados ever built. Displaced from mainline duties by the Poconos, they were certainly capable of work like this, heavy local freights with plenty of switching.

(Both, R. Chamberlin)

Above ▪ Its work done at Hackettstown, the huge Mike seems to slip its 63" drivers a bit getting started. The heavy Mikados had Delta cast trailing trucks rather than the fabricated trucks on the light Mikados in the 1200 series. These big 2-8-2s had been built to be the main line freight power for the railroad, but were quickly superceded by the 4-8-2s and 4-8-4s the Lackawanna bought in the prosperous late 1920s in the continuous quest to move the freight faster and more efficiently. Less versatile than the smaller engines, they were among the first to go as dieselization proceeded, so color shots of them in action are quite rare.

(R. Chamberlin)

Above ▪ The Hackettstown depot was a low and rambling building with a train order board. It looked like this on July 7, 1960. Hackettstown was once named Musconetcong, but the named was changed to honor local innkeeper Samuel Hackett, whose popularity reportedly rested on his custom of giving free drinks to all comers.

(Arthur Angstadt/Hawk Mountain Chapter NRHS collection)

Washington

Above ▪ Washington was the western terminus of local passenger trains to Hoboken, which reached the Hoboken Terminal by way of the Boonton Line through Paterson and Passaic. The trains used steam power almost exclusively until the end of steam in 1952/1953. In the years before dieselization, the locals were often led by older steam power that had been bumped from main line duty. One of the most interesting group of engines on the Lackawanna was the batch of 4-4-0s that lasted into the 1940s, well after most of their type had long been banished to the scrapyard. The Lackawanna's were deceptively modern in appearance, the result of rebuilding from center cab to end cab locomotives and receiving modern appliances. The Lackawanna was not the only anthracite road using 4-4-0s at this time; the D&H also had some assigned to locals out of Albany and Whitehall, New York. One of the Lackawanna's American types, the 978, was at Washington in 1941 in this fine portrait by William McChesney, one of the earliest railfans to shoot 35mm color shots of railroad subjects. Mr. McChesney was a native of Summit, New Jersey and grew up loving the Lackawanna, so it was natural that he ventured out several times in the prewar years to shoot his home railroad. It looks as if the crew of the local has agreed to pose for Mr. McChesney. *(William McChesney)*

Above ▪ The older power on the Washington runs was supplanted and eventually replaced by the Lackawanna's large group of Pacifics. The 119 is ready to head east with a morning local in 1941 on the 61-mile trip to Hoboken. The curving tracks by the depot join the Old Road with the line to Phillipsburg, which joins just out of sight to the right of the engine. Mr. McChesney wisely positioned the shot to show the classic Lackawanna lettering on the boxcar in the Washington freight yard. *(William McChesney)*

Cutoff

Above & Below ▪ Greendell was the first station west of Port Morris on the Cutoff. A freight has derailed by the tower, and a wreck train has come over from Port Morris to clean up the mess, led by F3 621C running solo. Greendell was 11.8 miles west of Port Morris. *(Both, Bill Hopping)*

Left ▪ The architectural gem of the Cutoff was Paulins Kill Viaduct at Hainesburg. The large concrete arch bridge spanned the stream of the same name and the Maybrook line of the Lehigh & New England, which connected at Hainesburg Junction with the New York, Susquehanna & Western. The bridge was 1,100 feet in length, and was the easternmost of the four big concrete arch bridges that shared the same general appearance; heading west, the next was at the crossing of the Delaware River at Slateford Junction, with the other two west of Scranton. All were steel-reinforced concrete structures. This is how the viaduct looked in April 1950, facing west with the Delaware Water Gap in the distance.

(Paul Reynolds)

Right ▪ One of the 1500-class Poconos was passing the lower quadrant semaphores near the Paulins Kill Viaduct in this pre-World War II shot by William McChesney. Bill McChesney was an early color slide pioneer taking much of his subjects in the early 1940s. His work is featured in *Trackside East of the Hudson 1941-1953* by this author and his son. *(William McChesney)*

Below ▪ Blairstown was the only station stop for passenger trains on the Cutoff. The town was named for John I. Blair, one of the founders of the consolidated Lackawanna in the 1860s. The station was in a section of the Cutoff where numerous deep cuts were made through the tops of ridges, affording photographers nice high angles that captured the look of the rolling hills of western New Jersey. One person who frequented the Blairstown vicinity for Lackawanna shots was Al Holtz, whose work around Blairstown was featured prominently in *Lackawanna Railroad in Color (Volume 1)* by Morning Sun. Here is another shot from Mr. Holtz's extensive work. The dogwoods are in bloom and the green of spring is starting to show as the PHOEBE SNOW accelerates west from the station stop at Blairstown. The Blairstown station can be seen in the background, to the left of the tracks. It's clear that the designers of the Cutoff had no great concern for serving local communities in this part of New Jersey; the station is the lone sign of human settlement in the scene. Blairstown proper was about two miles north of the isolated station. From this angle, it's apparent how well the Lackawanna's diesel passenger scheme matched the streamlined equipment, and just how handsome was a perfectly matched consist like this day's #3. *(Al Holtz)*

Above ▪ The Delaware River Bridge had the signature look of the Lackawanna in its glory years of construction before World War I, when cost was no object and the road gloried in the graceful concrete arch bridges built for the Cutoff project and the line reconstruction west of Scranton. A Pocono is heading over the bridge from Pennsylvania to New Jersey in August 1946, with a block of reefers behind the 4-8-4. This is how the scene appeared before I-80 was constructed on the New Jersey side of the river.

(R. Chamberlin)

Delaware River Bridge

Right ▪ The Pennsylvania side of the Delaware River Bridge was the better side to shoot trains. The bridge was angled to ease the connection of the Cutoff and the Old Road at Slateford Junction, affording excellent lighting for the afternoon passing of the eastbound PHOEBE SNOW. Train #6 was leaving Pennsylvania and heading down the Cutoff early in 1951, its matched equipment contrasting with the deep blue of the Delaware.

(Arthur Angstadt/Hawk Mountain Chapter NRHS collection)

Above ▪ Trailing a cloud of blue brake-shoe smoke, westbound #5, the TWILIGHT LIMITED, rolls across the Delaware bridge into the Water Gap as the caboose of a westbound train on the Old Road passes on the lower level. The TWILIGHT LIMITED was due into Slateford Junction at 5:31 PM, an ideal time to photograph it on summer afternoons. This shot was taken on August 3, 1952.

(Arthur Angstadt/Hawk Mountain Chapter NRHS collection)

Slateford Junction

Above ▪ At Slateford Junction the main line via the Cutoff was joined by the Old Road line by way of Washington, Oxford and Portland. The tower at Slateford Junction witnessed the westbound passage of a freight coming up the Old Road via Portland with 94 cars on Saturday, August 16, 1958. It's 5:07 PM, and the eastbound PHOEBE SNOW, train #6, passed the location just 10 minutes earlier. The train is heading off the Old Main's single track and merging with the double track main line just west of the Delaware River Bridge. H16-44 933 is the third unit out behind the 621-C and the 662-B; the trailing unit appears to be the 662-A. Trains on the Old Road often carried road switchers like the 933, probably heading to Scranton for shopping.

(Bill Hopping/Pat Lederer collection)

Above ▪ A ballast train headed off the Old Road and past the tower at Slateford Junction behind a double lashup of A/B/A F3 units in this undated photo, probably from the early 1950s. *(Marvin H. Cohen)*

RS3 913 was on the main line with a local freight in April 1954, with a wooden Lackawanna boxcar first out. The RS3 had been on the Lackawanna roster about two years, one of the fleet of freight road switchers that congregated around Port Morris and Bangor. This overhead angle shows how black road switchers accumulated a good coating of grime on all their horizontal surfaces and underframe. *(Dick Townley)*

Portland

Above ▪ Just south of the Delaware Water Gap on the west side of the river was the community of Portland, Pennsylvania. Portland was the point at which the Old Road met the Bangor & Portland Branch, a line that provided the Lackawanna access to the Cement Region of Northampton County. The Maybrook line of the Lehigh & New England crossed the Delaware River at Portland, and provided interchange with the Lackawanna just to the west of its bridge to New Jersey. A westbound freight was moving past the Portland depot, hidden from view by the Esso station, alongside the Delaware River after coming up the Old Road from Port Morris by way of Washington, and will soon join the main line at Slateford Junction to continue west on April 5, 1959. Portland was founded in 1845 by Captain James Ginn, a native of Portland, Maine, for which the town was named. By a curious coincidence, it was the Lackawanna's entrance to the cement district, whose product was christened Portland cement because it resembled building materials from the Isle of Portland in Great Britain. Portland itself was on the edge of the district, and did not share in the production of cement.
(Arthur Angstadt/Hawk Mountain Chapter NRHS collection)

Right, Center ▪ A spotless A/B/A set of passenger F3s has brought a fantrip special into Portland in May 1955. The shutterbugs are already unloading to get their shots of the train in perfect sunlight. *(Paul Reynolds)*

Right ▪ The Old Road crossed the Delaware River at Portland and followed the New Jersey shore of the river south through Manunka Chunk before heading to the east and south to Washington. The first community south of Portland on the New Jersey side was named Delaware. The Delaware station was built in 1887; it had waiting rooms, agent's office, and baggage room on the first floor and living quarters on the second floor. It was 70 feet from end to end, and torn down in the 1960s.
(Arthur Angstadt/Hawk Mountain Chapter NRHS collection)

Above ▪ Bangor was named for the city of the same name in North Wales, and it had the look of a Welsh mining town in this fine panoramic scene by Arthur Angstadt taken in June of 1951. This part of Pennsylvania was first a center of slate mining, then turned to cement in the early years of the 20th century. The area around Bangor was reputed to have pro-duced around two-thirds of all the country's slate, back when slate was the roofing material of choice. By the 1940s and 1950s, Bangor was as much a rail center as a mining town, with the Lackawanna's neat engine terminal and small yard alongside Martins Creek. The dominant feature of the Lackawanna in Bangor had to be the steeply elevated coal dock visible to the right of the train. The chunks of coal in those hoppers look about as big as telephones!

(Arthur Angstadt/Hawk Mountain Chapter NRHS collection)

Above ▪ Bangor was dreary and rainy on May 16, 1948 as 2-8-0 364 went about its work switching the yard. By 1950, 26 Consolidations were still on the Lackawanna roster. They dated back to the early years of the century, a period when this wheel arrangement dominated main line freight operations on most of the nation's railroads. Even by the stan-dards of their day the Lackawanna 2-8-0s were modest in size and power, producing only 34,197 pounds of tractive effort. Low drivered at 57" and straight boilered, the little engines were useful at switching and local freight duties around the system. The B&P was one of their last haunts, and a trip to Bangor in the 1940s or early 1950s usually found several at work. *(Theodore F. Gleichmann, Jr.)*

Above & Below ▪ Bangor Yard was the focal point of activity on the Bangor & Portland Branch. Not only was it still being switched by steam power in the early 1950s, the steam power was of museum quality antiquity. Old 2-8-0s performed both switching and local freight duties at Bangor and down the spider-web of Lackawanna lines in the cement district to the west and south. Bill Ellis visited Bangor in November 1952 and provides us with a look at the little Consolidations in the last fall of steam operations. The 367 was switching by the Bangor Lumber Company on November 4, 1952, and was joined by the 351. As the elderly steam kettles went about their chores, the nation's voters were turning out in record numbers to elect Dwight David Eisenhower to the first of his two terms as President. *(Both, William Ellis)*

Above & Below ▪ A pair of broadside views of the 367 shows the demure proportions of the 2-8-0. The borough of Bangor had the look of a mining town, with houses perched on hillsides overlooking the yard. *(William Ellis)*

Above = The big coal chute at Bangor provided a stern test for the elderly steamers assigned to spot loaded hoppers. With a nice assortment of company freight cars below the dock, the 367 slowly pushed cars up the structure. Judging by the B&O hopper ahead of the boxcar, this is bituminous coal and not anthracite. *(William Ellis)*

Right = The Bangor depot was a square, two-story affair that looked more like an old house than a railroad station. The Lackawanna's green and red paint scheme for structures was highly unusual, and seems especially bizarre on an atypical building like the depot at Bangor. The awnings, a true Pennsylvania touch, gave the old wooden building a touch of needed character, although we can't say much for the color coordination with the green of the building. This is how it looked on June 19, 1960. *(Arthur Angstadt/Hawk Mountain Chapter NRHS collection)*

Three of the Fairbanks-Morse H16-44s rest beside the Bangor engine house on July 3, 1959. Along with Alco RS3s, the 1,600 horsepower FMs replaced steam on the B&P in 1953 and were a fixture in the cement district well into the E-L era, ending up on the Chihuahua Pacifico Railroad in Mexico, a stronghold of Fairbanks-Morse power. *(Arthur Angstadt/Hawk Mountain Chapter NRHS collection)*

The Cement District

Above ▪ Lying south of Kittatinny Mountain – the local name of the Blue Ridge Mountain – and north and east of the Lehigh River in Northampton County, the Cement District of Pennsylvania was still rich in railroads in the 1950s. Tapping the cement trade in the region were lines of the Lehigh & New England and Lackawanna, the Lehigh Valley, and shortline Northampton & Bath. The Lackawanna headed south out of Bangor along Martins Creek to Martins Creek Junction, where one line continued along the path of the stream to the town of the same name. The longer of the two lines headed west along the south side of Kittatinny Mountain to Wind Gap, where it followed the path of the Little Bushkill Creek south to Nazareth and on to Bath. At Bath, a three-railroad town, it connected with the Northampton & Bath and L&NE. Although the region was dotted with cement quarries, it was part of the Pennsylvania Dutch country, and much of the countryside retained the neat and orderly look of this agricultural region. The region hosted one of the most memorable fantrips of the post-World War II years, a trip from Hoboken to the Cement Region in May 1949. The special left Hoboken on the Lackawanna, followed the Old Road to Washington, then headed over the Phillipsburg Branch and left Lackawanna tracks and followed the CNJ to Bethlehem, where it started up the Lehigh & New England to Bath and Pen Argyl. At Pen Argyl a stop was made to examine the Lehigh & New England's facilities, the center of activities on the L&NE and the location of its major shops. As always, the Lackawanna power for fantrips was washed and immaculate. Pocono 1641 posed at Pen Argyl beside a newer product of American Locomotive Company, L&NE FA1 709. This close-up shot shows just how handsome the final group of Poconos was, with a smooth boiler jacket and 74" Boxpok drivers. The curious design of the overhanging sand dome is readily apparent from this angle. The 1641 had been on the job 15 years when this shot was taken, not long for a steam engine but about what the builders of diesels advised their customers was the proper service life. The L&NE FA1s would not be able to test that theory on their home railroad. Delivered in 1947, the railroad itself would be gone in 1961, with the road's diesels sent to the L&N to work a few more years. Ironically, the Lackawanna, which had bought almost all its steam power from Alco, did not buy cab diesels like this from the Schenectady builder, preferring products from EMD, while the L&NE, which had been a loyal Baldwin customer in steam days, turned to Alco for its diesel fleet. A lot of shots of this trip have been published in various books and articles, but this is certainly one of the finest.

(Paul Reynolds)

Above ▪ November 4, 1952, was a busy day on the B&P. Bill Ellis found a location near Belfast Junction that provided a bucolic setting for the passage of Lackawanna Consolidations going about their work in this corner of the railroad. The 351 starts off the action, heading south nearing Belfast Junction with a solid train of cement hoppers returning for loading at the cement plants. *(William Ellis)*

Right ▪ After the 351 passed, the 362 took an eastbound freight back to Bangor. The Lackawanna had a large stable of Consolidations, dating back to the first decade of the 20th century, when the 2-8-0 type was the standard freight power on American railroads. The Lackawanna never pursued the huge drag-era Consolidations favored by other anthracite roads, although Port Morris was often home to the huge 90-class Consolidations of the Lehigh & Hudson River. The little 2-8-0s were useful in branch line duty, and lasted well into the 1950s in depleted but still significant numbers. There were originally 125 of these engines, numbered 351-399 and 724-799. In the confusing numbering approach that the Lackawanna seemed to love, the number of the engine was no real clue to its age relative to other engines of the same design.

(William Ellis)

Left ▪ A third Consolidation-powered freight showed up later that afternoon, this one heading west to Belfast Junction and Nazareth with the 365 bringing a solid block of cement cars for reloading. The Lackawanna had around 600 covered hoppers assigned to the cement business. Kittatinny Mountain's unbroken ridgeline can be seen in the background. *(William Ellis)*

Below ▪ The corn has been harvested and the trees on the hillsides are russet as the 365 steams down the line to Nazareth. In the background is a typical Pennsylvania Dutch farm, with white or gray the colors of choice for barns and outbuildings in this part of the Commonwealth. *(William Ellis)*

Right ▪ On September 20, 1952, Mikado 1250 was drifting westbound past the Lehigh Valley interchange at Belfast Junction on its way to Nazareth. The LV accessed the cement district on its Easton & Northern Branch from Easton, connecting with the L&NE at Stockertown and the Lackawanna at Belfast Junction. Cement was big business for the eastern roads until they lost the traffic to specially designed cement trucks in the late 1950s and 1960s. The 1200-series Mikados shared the work on the B&P with the 2-8-0s.

(William Ellis)

Below ▪ Inbound coal loads were an important part of the business of the Lackawanna in the cement district. Mikado 1236's train had five loads of black diamonds as it switched the lead at the Coplay Cement Company near Nazareth in October 1951.

*(Arthur Angstadt/
Hawk Mountain Chapter
NRHS collection)*

Delaware Water Gap

Above ■ Back on the main line west of Slateford Junction, we enter the famed Delaware Water Gap, where the Delaware River flows through a gap in the Blue Ridge – called here Kittatining Mountain – on its way south to Philadelphia and Delaware Bay. The Water Gap had made an impression on visitors since the mid-1800s, and was a favorite of romantic landscape painters like George Inniss of Morristown, New Jersey, who saw it as the ideal of the natural beauty that characterized America. The Lackawanna followed the twisting path of the river for two miles through the Gap, and it was always the scenic highlight of the trip over the Road of Scenic Beauty. It's not the scenery but the allure of a favored hot-dog stand along Route 611 that is getting the attention of the crewman on this eastbound freight in the Water Gap. On the New Jersey side of the river, one of the huge rock formations is visible, known to generations of college students from geology field trips to study the amazing natural history of the Northeast revealed in the mountainsides of the Water Gap. At one time the New York, Susquehanna & Western's light rails carried trains along the New Jersey side of the river enroute to their line to the anthracite country, but now the New Jersey side of the Gap is occupied by I-80. *(Bill Hopping)*

Above ■ Al Holtz was up in the cab of a westbound train as it entered the Water Gap at Slateford and passed an eastbound work train led by a single F unit. *(Al Holtz)*

Above ▪ The twin boroughs of Stroudsburg and East Stroudsburg are the gateway to the Poconos, and the Lackawanna did a thriving passenger business over the years at its Stroudsburg depot. It was actually in East Stroudsburg, but the Lackawanna just called it Stroudsburg, so we'll use the Lackawanna's name for the location. Located eight miles west of the Delaware Water Gap, Stroudsburg was the beginning of the really stiff gradient for westbound trains ascending the Poconos and a base for pushers waiting to assist westbound freights. The 1650, the Lackawanna's highest numbered Pocono, was in the region for which it was named, waiting at Stroudsburg on July 8, 1949 to back up and hook on to a waiting westbound train for the climb up to Pocono Summit. *(Arthur Angstadt/Hawk Mountain Chapter NRHS collection)*

Below ▪ On the morning of April 27, 1952 a three-unit set of Fs approached the Stroudsburg depot. The train is still a bit backlit, and the sharp low sun picks up the colors of the diesels' Lackawanna freight scheme nicely.

(Arthur Angstadt/Hawk Mountain Chapter NRHS collection)

Above ■ One of the most unusual passenger trains to grace Lackawanna rails waits for the eastbound PHOEBE SNOW at Stroudsburg in 1951. This is the Pennsylvania Railroad's train between Stroudsburg and Trenton, using the Lackawanna between Stroudsburg and the connection of the Old Road with an extension from the PRR's Belvidere-Delaware Branch to the Lackawanna at Manunka Chunk. In the days before most people traveled to vacation spots by automobile, the PRR trains were well patronized and usually ran behind K-4 Pacifics. By the 1950s, the demand was minimal for trains #585/586, with a Pennsy gas-electric car usually assigned to the Sunday-only operation. This day an Alco switcher was sufficient to haul a single car for the few patrons down the Delaware River valley to New Jersey's capital city, with connections there to major cities on the Northeast Corridor line.

(Arthur Angstadt/Hawk Mountain Chapter NRHS collection)

Below ■ By 1960, heavier trains and years of service made it necessary to build larger and larger blocks of F units to keep the trains moving. A westbound freight is getting underway at Stroudsburg with two FT units assisting an A/B/B/A set of F3s on the Pocono grade.

(Arthur Angstadt/Hawk Mountain Chapter NRHS collection)

Fall colors are just beginning to show on September 25, 1955 as the tower operator at S Tower in Stroudsburg hoops up orders to the fireman of an eastbound freight
about to cross Analomink Street. The train has finished the steepest part of the descent
from the crest of the Poconos and in less than 10 miles will be in the Delaware Water Gap.
Arthur Angstadt's luck was good this day, getting full sun on the train and dark clouds for contrast,
the dramatic sort of sky that comes mostly in the autumn months. Stroudsburg Tower was the last
DL&W tower to remain open west of New Jersey, lasting well into the Conrail years.

(Arthur Angstadt/Hawk Mountain Chapter NRHS collection)

The Pocono Mountains

Above ▪ At Analomink, around four miles west of Stroudsburg, a pair of Lackawanna road switchers, RS3 903 and a Train Master, is preparing to shove a westbound freight in June 1958.
(Arthur Angstadt/Hawk Mountain Chapter NRHS collection)

Above ▪ Henry's Crossing was a remote location on the Pocono grade, south of Cresco. On October 18, 1960 two Train Masters have been assigned the task of pushing a westbound freight up the grade. The hard work has nicely weathered the trucks of the FMs with sand applied to keep adhesion on the long climb up to Pocono Summit.
(Arthur Angstadt/Hawk Mountain
Chapter NRHS collection)

Left ▪ Solid gray Phase I F3 656 led an A/B/B/A set of F units slowly around the big curve at Cresco at 4:05 PM on Sunday, May 8, 1959 with a big westbound train of 121 cars. Cresco is the point at which the line changes from a compass north by northwest direction to a south by west orientation. This set of F units includes each of the three schemes that Lackawanna Fs wore. The somber appearance of the all-gray 656 contrasts with the dirty, but still colorful, freight garb on the first B unit, and the passenger scheme of the trailing F3A. Lacking both the yellow nose and the maroon stripes, the small number of F units in the dip scheme was out of character for a railroad that had always prided itself on appearances. Happily, the experiment was deemed unsuccessful, and the road standardized instead on the single wide-striped passenger scheme. *(Bill Hopping)*

Above ▪ Heading west at Cresco on July 8, 1949, was this steam/diesel double header. F3 658 is doing what it was bought to do, helping trains up the heavy Pocono grades, leading a hard-working Pocono past the curved Cresco station platforms in the brief period when a lucky railfan could find steam and diesel working in tandem. As any motive power man can tell you, it made a lot more sense to have the diesel leading the steam engine, not inhaling its smoke in the trailing position. *(Arthur Angstadt/Mike Del Vecchio collection)*

Above ▪ West of Cresco, the line passed by Seven Pines Mountain and crossed Devils Hole Creek. The Lackawanna in the Devils Hole area climbed high on a fill. It was one of the areas hardest hit by the rains and subsequent mudslides that devastated the Poconos on August 19, 1955. Hurricane Diane turned inland and dumped a deluge of rain on the Poconos, causing streams to cascade over their banks and wash away roads, homes, and about 75 miles of the Lackawanna. The reconstruction work was still underway but the trains were running again in September. It cost the Lackawanna around $13.5 million in lost revenues and reconstruction costs to put the railroad back together again. A westbound ascended the grade on September 25, 1955 behind the 621A. *(Arthur Angstadt/Hawk Mountain Chapter NRHS collection)*

West of the Summit

Above ▪ West of Pocono Summit, the Lackawanna passed through a surprisingly level terrain around Tobyhanna and Gouldsboro before returning to hillier surroundings near Moscow and the curving descent to the Lackawanna Valley at Scranton. This is a cold, high mountaintop area, dotted with lakes and ponds. Tobyhanna, Indian for "dark waters," is 1,933 feet above sea level, 1,510 feet higher than the elevation of Stroudsburg. Arthur Angstadt captured the feel of the summit of the Poconos well in his shot of a westbound freight curving past a small pond just east of Tobyhanna as it passes under Route 611 on March 20, 1959. By the calendar, it's the last day of winter, but the green of spring will not be seen in these high elevations for several more weeks. *(Arthur Angstadt /Hawk Mountain Chapter NRHS collection)*

Above ▪ At Moscow, 39 miles west of Stroudsburg and a little over 12 miles east of Scranton, an eastbound freight is ascending the west slope of the Poconos, following the path etched by Roaring Brook on its way down to the Susquehanna from the heights of the Moosic Mountains. It's mostly loaded coal on its way up the hill this day, with two F3As pushing hard on the steel caboose. Route 435 is on the right, a road well known to railfans chasing specials and trains from Steamtown up Moosic Mountain from Scranton to Moscow.

(Bill Hopping)

SCRANTON

In the early years of the anthracite boom, the only town of any size on the upper Susquehanna River in Pennsylvania was Wilkes-Barre. Most of the region was still wilderness, heavily wooded and mountainous, lacking in transportation and largely unpopulated, even though it was close in miles to major urban centers like New York and Philadelphia. As the rock coal ignited the first wave of industrialization in the country, entrepreneurs from outside the region looked to it as the source of the natural resources needed to produce high-quality iron. Besides anthracite, northeastern Pennsylvania had nearby sources of iron ore, and the hard coal burned so hot compared to other fuels that it produced a better-quality iron than had been possible before in the United States. One family lured to the Lackawanna Valley in search of iron and coal was the Scrantons. George and Selden Scranton operated the Oxford Iron Works in Oxford, New Jersey, in the western part of the state. In 1842 Selden's father-in-law William Henry persuaded them to invest in his iron-manufacturing venture in the wilds of the Lackawanna River Valley, north of Wilkes-Barre. Borrowing heavily from relatives and outsiders, the Scrantons bought out Henry and began making nails, then took the major risk of shifting to the construction of rails for railways. At this time, in the 1840s, all rails were being made in England and were shipped to America. Costs were high, and availability often did not meet the demand from the fast-growing American rail system. The opportunity to make a fortune was there for the taking, but the Scrantons had to go heavily in debt to meet the timetable demanded of their first and then only customer, the New York and Erie (the latter-day Erie). They met their deadline with four days to spare, and built up a growing trade in the sought-after iron rails, incorporating their Lackawanna Iron and Coal Company in 1853. Curiously, the Lackawanna owed its existence largely to its success in providing the rails for its long-time rival and eventual merger partner, the Erie.

The biggest logistical problem in meeting the Erie contract was the lack of good transportation, so the Scrantons wisely supported the building of two railroads, one north from the new community they named after themselves to connect with the Erie, the other east and south to the Delaware River at Stroudsburg. These lines became the basis of the Delaware, Lackawanna & Western, and established the city of Scranton as the heart of the railroad, a role it played right to the end of the Lackawanna's independent existence.

The Scrantons used the land they bought from William Henry to build a major new city where Roaring Brook emptied into the Lackawanna River, right atop coal deposits that allowed mining almost within sight of the downtown areas. The railroad was another major source of jobs for the city, and Scranton took off, growing to a city of 45,000 residents by 1880 and eclipsing in size and economic importance its downriver rival, Wilkes-Barre.

Unlike the capitalists of Wilkes-Barre, who made their fortunes exclusively from the ownership of coal lands and mines, the Scrantons were interested in diversifying the economy of their new community. As historians Donald L. Miller and Richard E. Sharpless noted, "they [the Scrantons] were venture capitalists willing to take enormous risks and not simply transfixed by coal…they built industry but also a city and endowed it with parks, a hospital, a library, and modern urban services. Though aggressive defenders of their order and interests, they made a place for others." Through the leadership of the Scrantons, the Lackawanna was centered in a city with a population base and industry that provided it with more traffic than just the hard coal that lay beneath the surface of the Lackawanna Valley. It had textile mills, and until it relocated to Buffalo, the Lackawanna Iron & Steel Company, the successor to the original iron business started by the Scrantons.

Right ▪ *Trains Magazine* ran a feature story by John T. Cunningham on the Lackawanna, in which the author said "if Hoboken can be called the head of the Lackawanna Railroad, Scranton can be called its heart — particularly from the standpoint of freight." Scranton was the so-called "Capital of the Coal Region" and the fourth largest city in Pennsylvania, with a population of almost 150,000 residents in the peak years of the anthracite industry. Scranton was the location of the company's major shops, and the center of its freight operations. You didn't have to go far in the city to see evidence of the Lackawanna's presence in Scranton. The city was also served by the Jersey Central, the Erie, the Delaware & Hudson, and the Laurel Line, an electric interurban line. But it was first and foremost a Lackawanna town. On May 3, 1952 RS3 912 was heading into Scranton with a westbound roustabout at the Harrison Avenue viaduct. The 912 was brand-new in 1952, part of an order for eight of the 1,600 horsepower road switchers to complement the 10 already on the roster. It looks as if the Alco product is already having some problems, judging from the open door on the fireman's side revealing the 244 prime mover. The black paint of the engine has picked up a good deal of grime already, and this overhead view shows how it sticks to the top of the hood and cab and running boards. It's surely a candidate for the engine washer at Scranton. Harrison, in honor of President William Henry Harrison, was the name not only of the street, but was also one of the many names for the city before it settled on Scranton; the community was known at various times as Unionville, Skunk's Misery, Slocum Hollow, Harrison, and Scrantonia. *(William Ellis)*

Right ▪ An A/A pair of FTs is on the east side of Scranton. The imposing bulk of Scranton's six-story passenger station dominates the scene to the right. It looks like the PHOEBE SNOW is making its stop at the station. The Lackawanna & Wyoming Valley tracks can be seen below the station at a much lower level, heading to South Scranton and Wilkes-Barre. This shot clearly shows how Scranton is situated in a bowl, with mountains hemming it in to the east and west, a problem that dogged the Lackawanna throughout its history and necessitated helper service both east and west of the city.

(Mike Del Vecchio collection)

Left ▪ Scranton generated a good deal of passenger business for the railroad, enough to justify a set of Hoboken/Scranton passenger trains Monday through Saturday, and numerous passenger extras, especially baseball extras in the summer months to New York Yankee games. The Scranton station at Jefferson Street between Spruce Street and Lackawanna Avenue was a magnificent symbol of the railroad in Scranton, built in 1908. It was built of Indiana limestone and designed by architects Edward Langley of Scranton and Kenneth Murchison of New York. Travelers using the station were impressed by the 36 mosaic murals illustrating the history of the Lackawanna. The umbrella platforms are coming in handy this rainy day in the late 1940s as one of the 1934-built Poconos makes the station stop at Scranton with a milk train. These 4-8-4s were equipped with 74" drivers, midway between the 77" of the 1500s and the 70" drivers of the first two groups of 1600s, making them equally at home on freight and passenger trains. *(Frank Watson)*

Scranton Station

Above ▪ The Laurel Line's Scranton depot was adjacent to the Lackawanna passenger station, at a lower level along Cedar Street. It terminated with a sharp loop that allowed cars to change directions. After passenger service was ended, the line continued to use the nearby freight yard for the duration of its existence. Lackawanna EMD switcher 533 and GE 44-tonner 51 switched the L&WV interchange on September 26, 1953 with the impressive Lackawanna station in the background. *(William Ellis)*

Steam Switchers

Above ▪ The Lackawanna's 0-8-0s were uncommonly handsome steam switchers. Well-proportioned and rugged in appearance, they were a great investment by the railroad, which built them at Scranton Shops using the boilers and whatever else useful they could salvage from 4-6-2s and 2-8-2s made surplus in the 1920s and 1930s by the purchase of more modern steam road power. Used mostly in switching duties, they could also take local freights and transfers over the line. They congregated in large numbers in the city of their birth. The 205 was at the engine terminal at Scranton on September 27, 1952. Note the different placement of the headlight and bell on the 205 and the 0-8-0 behind it.

(Marvin H. Cohen)

Below, Left ▪ The 238 was on the lower level tracks at Scranton in September 1947. The yard below the passenger station was used both by the Lackawanna and the Lackawanna & Wyoming Valley. Known by its nickname, the Laurel Line, this was an electric line that handled both interurban passenger and freight business between Scranton and Wilkes-Barre. *(Frank Watson)*

Right ▪ Two of the ubiquitous 0-8-0s have picked up loads from the Diamond Hill colliery in the north side of Scranton, and are near Lackawanna Avenue on the Diamond Hill Branch for clearance to enter the main line. This branch joined the main line west of the passenger station and east of Bridge 60. The Northern Anthracite Field, which provided all of the Lackawanna's coal business, was also the most concentrated and richest of the several coal fields in the anthracite region. This meant that the Lackawanna had only short branches from the main line to the coal mines, unlike the Lehigh Valley and the Reading, which were forced to extend spider webs of coal branches through their fields in Carbon, Schuylkill and Luzerne counties to the south of the Lackawanna. Scranton was able to serve as both the collecting point for most of the coal, and also the operational and maintenance center for the main line of the railroad. Although the DL&W never approached the anthracite loadings of the Reading, accounting usually for about 12-16% of the total for the region, it was in most ways the most cost-efficient and streamlined of the five major anthracite carriers, with only the Delaware & Hudson comparable in its ability to combine coal operations with main line freight and passenger activities. *(William Ellis)*

Above ▪ Beautiful low light suffused 0-8-0 215 in August 1953 as it sat by the coal dock at Scranton. The powerful switch engine has had her last fire go out, as steam operations have ended on the Lackawanna. The stack is covered and the end is near. It's time to marvel one last time at the touches that made the Lackawanna 0-8-0s so special: the aluminum-painted smokebox, the graceful curvature of the boiler, the red-painted cab windows. *(Paul Reynolds)*

Above ▪ The bleakness of the anthracite region was always most evident on winter days, when patches of old snow partly covered the culm piles and mine tailings, and black hoppers and engines went about their work in the dingy mining towns and railroad yards under a leaden sky. Kids learned young how to hop aboard a slow-moving coal train and rescue enough slabs of anthracite to keep the family warm for another winter night. On Washington's Birthday, February 22, 1952, winter has its embrace firmly in place as 0-8-0 235 plods over Keyser Valley Road with loaded coal hoppers. This is between Hampton Yard and Cayuga Junction on the Keyser Valley Branch. This important line of the Lackawanna branched off the Bloomsburg Line at Taylor and looped around to the north and west to rejoin the main line at Cayuga Junction on the grade leading west out of Scranton. *(William Ellis)*

Above ▪ About as different an engine from the big 200s as you could imagine was the little 0-4-0T #7 that switched the Scranton shops. The 7 was built by Baldwin in 1922, and was obviously too light for any duties other than shop switcher duty. Frank Watson found the 7 on the Scranton turntable in July 1947, with a smoking Pocono as background. *(Frank Watson)*

Tank Engines

Left ▪ What's this, a tank engine with a tender? The 120 was switching a tender at the Scranton Shop in July 1947. The 120 was built as an 0-6-0 in 1908 by Alco, and was converted to a tank engine in 1928. Operating in the protected environs of the shops, it lasted until the end of steam in 1953. *(Frank Watson)*

Poconos at Scranton

Above ▪ The 1505 sat cold at Scranton in the winter of 1947. The snow that has accumulated on the tender and atop the 1927-build 4-8-4 is an indication that the end of the 1505's active service life has arrived. Looking at the 1505, it's clear how far the Poconos evolved from their start with the five 1500s. The first of the Poconos were pioneers of their engine type, and looked rather old-fashioned with their small tender and spoked driving wheels. They were among the first of the modern Lackawanna power to be scrapped; all were off the roster before 1950.

(Frank Watson)

Above ▪ In a fine shot of Lackawanna steam in winter, the imposing bulk of one of the 1929-built Poconos contrasts with the white snow and steam as it starts an eastbound coal drag near the Scranton Station in 1947. These freight Poconos had lower drivers than the 1500s that preceded them, but their most unusual spotting feature was the unusual front-end treatment given them after rebuilding. The smokebox was extended, a Worthington feedwater heater was installed, and the headlight was mounted at the top of the smokebox, similar to the headlight arrangement of the Scranton 0-8-0s. Without any numberplate or logo on the smokebox, they had a curious and rather ungainly look compared to the other Poconos, looking almost as if they were lurching or leaning forward. *(Frank Watson)*

Left ▪ Steam and diesel engines working together on a train was one of the most exciting events to witness in the steam-to-diesel transition period even though this slide is a bit "fuzzy." Lancaster native Jim Shuman was on hand at Scranton on September 1, 1947 as a coal train headed east behind one of the modern 1934-built Poconos as road engine and brand-new F3 helpers on the head end. The crew of the 656 has already discovered the virtues of EMD's early air-conditioning system – open the nose door to let the air-flow cool off the cab. The 656 A/B was delivered in January of 1947 with low gearing for duty like this. This is, of course, the proper way to run a steam/diesel pairing, with the diesel up front to avoid sucking in all the smoke from the steam engine's exhaust on the long, slow climb up the Poconos. *(James P. Shuman)*

Above ▪ On March 9, 1952, the Lackawanna was still running steam/diesel combinations, but this time the order was reversed and Pocono 1641 has been assigned the helper duty. It is heading west at Bridge 60, assisting F7 631-A on the climb out of Scranton to Clarks Summit. In the short distance between Bridge 60 and Clarks Summit, the line climbs from an elevation of 741' to 1,240'. The Bloomsburg Branch tracks diverge in the foreground, leading to Taylor Yard, Kingston, and ultimately the end of the line at Northumberland. Bridge 60 carried the Lackawanna tracks over the Lackawanna River and main line of the D&H. It was so named because it is 60 miles west of the Delaware River crossing. *(William Ellis)*

Engine Washing

Above ▪ The Lackawanna seemed to do everything with class, and appearance of their equipment was an important consideration. To keep their engines clean, they utilized this engine washer at Scranton. Even workaday engines like 0-8-0 225 received the treatment, with the dramatic results recorded by Art Angstadt on October 14, 1951. This area was normally off-limits to photographers, so it was a treat to be shown the wash rack in operation during the centennial festivities.

(Arthur Angstadt/Hawk Mountain Chapter NRHS collection)

Right, Top ▪ Once the 225 was cleaned, it was the turn of the 1233. The Mikado is being backed through the high-pressure spray, its bell clanging to warn the workmen of its reverse move. It's not really all that dirty by the standards of many railroads, but the Lackawanna kept them as clean as a whistle. Mr. Angstadt seemed to be fascinated by locomotive washing. In *Trackside around Allentown, PA 1947-1968 with Arthur Angstadt*, the Morning Sun book featuring his photography in the Lehigh Valley, his pictures of diesels being washed at the CNJ's Bethlehem Engine Terminal are reminiscent of these earlier images at Scranton.

(Arthur Angstadt/Hawk Mountain Chapter NRHS collection)

Right ▪ The water cascades off the flanks of the 1233, as steam and spray combine to form a beautiful fountain of white against the clear blue October sky. The huge coal dock at the Scranton facility is visible at the right of the picture.

(Arthur Angstadt/Hawk Mountain Chapter NRHS collection)

Centennial Celebration

Above ▪ Both the Erie and the Lackawanna celebrated centennial events in 1951. The Erie staged its highly successful recreation of the first run linking the Hudson River and the Great Lakes in 1851. The Lackawanna celebrated the centennial year of its existence, fittingly with a celebration at Scranton, where the road's long history began. Railfans like Mr. Angstadt traveled to Scranton on October 14, 1951 as the Lackawanna opened its Scranton facilities to celebrate the centennial year. The star of the show was Mother Hubbard 4-4-0 4, painted in the gaudy colors of the 19th century. Take a good look at this engine. Forget the age and the bright paint: this is one big, powerful locomotive!

(M. Del Vecchio collection)

Right ▪ Little shop switcher 120 was shined up and under steam for the visitors to the Scranton facilities on October 14, 1951. The 0-6-0T tank engine was a fixture around Scranton, and was often spiffed up like this for special occasions.

(Arthur Angstadt/Hawk Mountain Chapter NRHS collection)

Diesels at Scranton

Above ▪ The 652 A/B set rests at the Scranton engine terminal on September 27, 1952. This set was among the low-geared FTs bought for helper service both east and west of Scranton. Built in 1945, by 1952 it has received some subtle changes: the roofs of the units have been painted black, and the distinctive red light has been added on the nose door. The smooth bulldog nose of the FT has not been altered with nose MU connections or additional grab irons, nor do the units have the long grab irons over the windshield that later EMD cab units featured. *(Marvin H. Cohen)*

Above ▪ Three of the rare prewar diesels on the Lackawanna roster were together at Scranton. The 408 was an Alco HH-600 built at Schenectady in 1933, in the rather crude design Alco used for its early "high-hood" end cab switchers. The 454 hooked up behind it is even rarer, a center-cab switcher produced by General Electric and Ingersoll-Rand at roughly the same time as the 408. The 409 in the right background was a relative youngster by comparison, an HH-660 built in 1940 with the more modern high-hood design. *(Bill Hopping)*

Above ▪ Hurricane Diane's fury was two weeks in the past by Saturday, September 3, 1955, but the damage to the Lackawanna's main line in the Poconos still required its trains to detour over the Lehigh Valley. Coming into Pittston Junction is Train #2, the eastbound POCONO EXPRESS, with E8s 817 and 818 on the lead. The train is on the Lackawanna's Bloomsburg Branch, and will soon be heading up the tracks to the left, the Mountain Cutoff of the LV, going in the opposite direction after turning at the wye at Pittston Junction. The train is paralleling South Main Street in Duryea, north of Pittston, near the Coxton Road crossing. *(Edward S. Miller)*

Right ▪ The eastbound PHOEBE SNOW has backed over the Lackawanna River bridge and changed direction, and is proceeding east again over the bridge to start the run over the Lehigh Valley on September 3, 1955. Although Edward Miller came here to shoot the Lackawanna detours, this was a location he frequented with great success over the years, as witness his magnificent shots of the New York, Ontario & Western freights entering Coxton Yard featured in Morning Sun's *New York, Ontario & Western in Color. (Edward S. Miller)*

Above ▪ At Pittston Junction, the westbound PHOEBE SNOW has returned to Lackawanna tracks and is about to head north to Scranton to rejoin the main line for the trip to Buffalo. Pittston Tower in the background controlled the movements at this busy junction that was used to seeing the top trains of the Lehigh Valley bang over the diamond, but not Lackawanna streamliners like this. *(Edward S. Miller)*

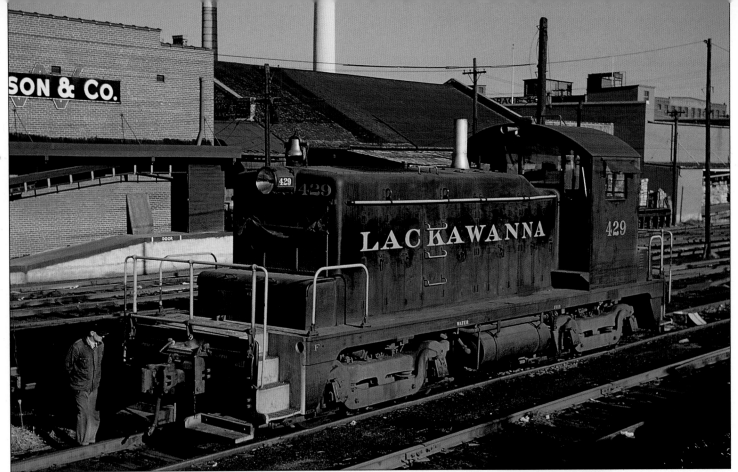

Above ▪ The Lackawanna & Wyoming Valley Railroad was a 19-mile electrified line between the cities of Scranton and Wilkes-Barre, the two largest urban centers in Northeast Pennsylvania. It opened for business in 1903, and operated for a half-century, longer than most interurban operations. Known as the *Laurel Line*, it handled freight as well as passenger traffic. Passenger service ended on the last day of December 1952, but freight service continued for some time thereafter. The line had used an electric locomotive, number 401, for its freight operations, using a third rail for power. The end of passenger service made the third rail electric operation infeasible to keep running for the small amount of freight business that remained, so the line relied upon leased Lackawanna diesel switchers until it ceased operation. Lackawanna SW1 429 was on lease to the Laurel Line on December 5, 1953 when Edward Miller found it working at the L&WV yard at Wilkes-Barre. Look closely to see the metal apparatus added to the top of the cab roof, to trip the traffic lights in Wilkes-Barre, something required on all the Lackawanna engines leased to the Laurel Line. *(Edward S. Miller)*

Left ▪ On Saturday, July 2, 1955, SW1 434 was heading north on the Laurel Line at Hughestown, near Pittston. It is passing through the location of the Butler Colliery alongside U. S. Route 11, visible to the right of the train. The shot captures the feel of the anthracite region, although by 1955 mining was in decline. Edward Miller, the great chronicler of the Laurel Line, made this shot and many more fine shots recording the final years of the L&WV. (See the book *Trackside around Scranton, Pa. 1952-1976 with Edward S. Miller* by Chuck Yungkurth.) Compare this shot with the shot of bright-red electric combine 114 heading south in the same location in Morning Sun's *Pennsylvania Trolleys in Color Volume I*. *(Edward S. Miller)*

Left ▪ Taylor Yard and the community of Taylor where it was located were named for Moses Taylor, a Lackawanna director in the mid-1800s. Taylor Yard was located three and one- half miles south of Scranton, where the Keyser Valley Branch and the Bloomsburg Branch joined at the Taylor Wye. Taylor Yard was a collection point for deadlined engines in the years of dieselization after World War II. Consolidation 796 sat forlornly at Taylor before scrapping in October 1947. Check out the wood Lackawanna USRA boxcar on the adjacent track. The white dot on the boxcar indicated it was assigned to less-than-carload (lcl) service. *(Frank Watson)*

Above ▪ Southwest of Taylor, the Northeast Extension of the Pennsylvania Turnpike crosses the Bloomsburg Branch, the Lackawanna River, and the CNJ/D&H main line between Scranton and Wilkes-Barre. An EMD switcher was working hard on the Bloomsburg Branch far below, pushing the cars northbound judging from the direction of the blue smoke plume from the switcher. The houses in the background are in the borough of Old Forge. This shot shows how narrow the valley of the Lackawanna is, with high mountains on both sides of the river.

(Arthur Angstadt/Hawk Mountain Chapter NRHS collection)

Kingston

Right ▪ The Lackawanna River empties into the Susquehanna at Pittston. At Pittston Junction, the Lackawanna crossed the passenger line of the Lehigh Valley at grade, near the east end of Coxton Yard where the LV's passenger line met the Mountain Cutoff, the route taken by LV freight up and out of the Wyoming Valley. The Bloomsburg Branch crossed the Susquehanna at Pittston and followed the course of the river on its north bank. At Kingston, across the river from Wilkes-Barre, a small yard permitted the Lackawanna to put together coal trains. Kingston was a good-sized community, with a population around 21,000 at the time of these shots, and had three working coal mines. In the 1940s the anthracite business was still an important part of the Lackawanna's business, around 20% of the freight tonnage, and Kingston was a busy spot. Frank Watson visited Kingston on a cold winter afternoon in 1947. The low light was probably right at the margins for shooting slow early Kodachrome film, but Mr. Watson was able to record some memorable images that far-off day. Consolidation 735 was switching at the north end of the yard, near the lower-quadrant semaphore signals. Check out the pole next to the caboose! *(Frank Watson)*

Above ▪ Getting closer to the tracks, Frank used the low sun angle to full advantage to shoot a going-away shot of the 735 hard at work at Kingston. *(Frank Watson)*

Right ▪ Along with the five original Poconos, perhaps the most elusive subjects for color photography were the 4-8-2s. One of the Mountains has hooked on to an eastbound coal train at Kingston, and the sidelighting shows the look of these powerful machines. *(Frank Watson)*

Above ■ Blasting a perfect plume of smoke skyward, 4-8-2 2224 assists an eastbound coal train leaving Kingston Yard in the winter of 1947. In deference to the raw power of the Mountain, the wood caboose has been placed behind the pusher for the climb up and over the Poconos. *(Frank Watson)*

Above ■ Pocono 1628, one of the third group of 4-8-4s built by Alco in 1932, was passing the tower at Kingston with a hopper train on that winter day in 1947. These engines, the 1621-1630, had 70" drivers like the 1929-built 1600s, but had a more pleasing look, with the headlight centered on the smokebox. Winters can be quite severe in Pennsylvania's northeastern corner, and it looks like a cold, clear day that requires dedication for a photographer to brave. The tower operator is probably working especially hard in the cold weather to throw the switches on the Armstrong levers indicated by the rods in the foreground. *(Frank Watson)*

Where else did you find men in suits and engineer's caps but a railroad fantrip in the 1940s or 1950s? The Lackawanna was a willing host for many trips, including a tour of the line to Northumberland in September 1956. At Northumberland, where the West and North Branches of the Susquehanna River meet, the Lackawanna connected with the Pennsylvania's Harrisburg to Buffalo line. In 1956, Northumberland was a mecca for steam enthusiasts, with the roundhouse there still alive with the sounds and smells of working steam on one of the last outposts of steam power on the Pennsylvania. The PRR obliged the fans by positioning the 5141 alongside the F3s of the special. The Bloomsburg Branch from Northumberland east to Berwick has been saved from abandonment, and is now operated by the North Shore Railroad, which uses the old freighthouse in Northumberland as its center of operations.

(Paul Reynolds)

Clarks Summit

Above ▪ Our side trip down the Bloomsburg Branch completed, let's head out of Scranton westbound on the main line. Westbound trains leaving Scranton had a stiff 7-mile grade out of the Lackawanna Valley up to Clarks Summit, with a maximum gradient of 1.6%. The grade required the use of helpers on most westbound freights. The community of Clarks Summit was a pleasant suburb of Scranton, seemingly removed from the gritty reality of the coal towns not far away in the valley. In what looks to be an aerial photograph, but in actuality was taken from the high bridge that carries the Northeast Extension of the Pennsylvania Turnpike over the tracks at Clarks Summit, the eastbound PHOEBE SNOW was racing down the hill to Scranton on October 4, 1960, with three head-end cars marring the otherwise matched look of the train. This view today is very different, with trees blocking much of the view of the tracks and the usual all-American strip replacing the rural look along U. S. Route 6 visible in the background.

(William Echternacht/NRHS collection)

Above ▪ The Lackawanna managed to hang on to the milk business well through the 1950s and even into the early years of the Erie-Lackawanna. The region of central New York State served by the branches to Syracuse and Utica is one of the greatest dairying areas of the country, and milk was the life's-blood of many of the communities along the Lackawanna. The milk cars were collected at Binghamton and assembled into #44 eastbound for Hoboken via the Boonton Line. Its westbound counterpart was #47, seen here climbing the grade to Clarks Summit behind a pair of the passenger F3s on August 2, 1958.
(William Ellis)

Right ▪ An E-L shot finds the eastbound ERIE-LACKAWANNA LIMITED passing the station at Factoryville, west of Clarks Summit, in August 1961. The track still looks maintained to Lackawanna standards, and the train looks quite a bit like the PHOEBE SNOW, but the E-L decal on the nose of the lead E unit is a giveaway that times have changed. The new road, dominated at first by an Erie management team, dropped the magical name for the new road's top train, and ran a pathetic Buffalo section of the New York-Chicago LIMITED for a while with the name PHOEBE SNOW. Under the leadership of former Lackawanna chief executive William White in the mid-1960s the PHOEBE SNOW name was resurrected for the second time, but as a New York to Chicago train. *(William Ellis)*

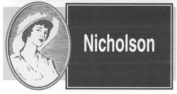

Nicholson

Above ▪ Very little prepared one for the first sight of the Tunkhannock Viaduct at the small community of Nicholson, 19 miles west of Scranton. Soaring 240 feet above Tunkhannock Creek and the village of Nicholson, the structure dwarfed any other reinforced concrete bridge when it opened for traffic on November 7, 1915. Almost a half-mile in length, the viaduct was the key to the 39.6 mile Cutoff between Clarks Summit and Hallstead. This was the view of the viaduct that greeted travelers heading north on the Lackawanna Trail, U. S. Route 11, as they headed around the curve into Nicholson and beheld the huge bridge in the twilight of a winter day in 1950. Much of the route of U. S. 11 followed the old right-of-way of the Lackawanna, which was largely replaced after the line was relocated as part of the upgrading that included the construction of the viaduct and its smaller look-alike farther north at Martins Creek, also known as the Kingsley Bridge. Construction of the viaduct began in 1912, with the company of Flickwir and Bush, Inc. the chief contractors. A narrow gauge railroad was laid at the base of the bridge to bring in the building materials. Three towers were constructed, one at each end of the valley and one at the center point, to support cables over which the buckets of wet cement were moved to drop the cement into the large forms of structural steel and wood for the arches. It was a triumph for the fledgling cement industry as well as the railroad; all told, it required 4,509,000 cubic feet of concrete to finish the graceful span, considered by many to be the most beautiful bridge in America.

(Paul Reynolds)

Above ▪ Nicholson's passenger depot was on the west side of the viaduct, and was a neat tiled-roof structure built as part of the Cutoff project. The viaduct is out of sight behind the train and station as three-portholed Phase I F3 605C leads a mixed consist of an F7B, Train Master 860 and an F7A west with a 64-car train at 1:39 PM on Thursday, May 30, 1957.

(Bill Hopping/Pat Lederer collection)

Binghamton

The westbound PHOEBE SNOW was making its station stop at Binghamton in an undated photograph. The cars look like late 1940s or earlier models, and the F3s look new, so this may be the LACKAWANNA LIMITED rather than the PHOEBE SNOW. The Italianate clock tower of the Lackawanna station is out of sight to the right, blocked by the water tank to the right of the shot. The Erie and Lackawanna had side-by-side stations in Binghamton, and the Erie is not shy about announcing its presence, with a large neon sign at the walkway down to its station from the Chenango Street bridge. The Lackawanna station was by far the finer of the two Binghamton stations, with a lunch room and large waiting room, while the Erie's rambling one-story red station, at the left of the tracks in this shot, had none of the elegance of its competitor's. *(Marvin H. Cohen)*

Left, Top ▪ The lead F3 is flying white flags as a passenger extra heads east out of the Binghamton passenger station in April 1959. *(J. J. Young)*

Left, Bottom ▪ The adjacent open-sided bridges carried the Lackawanna and the Erie over the Chenango River, just west of the passenger stations. This area was a favorite location for photographers. A pair of E8s led by the 817 takes the westbound PHOEBE SNOW over the Chenango in June of 1959. The bridge itself was a plate girder bridge, but the Lackawanna's penchant for concrete shows in the bridge approach emblazoned with the date of its construction, 1910. The Lackawanna didn't have much longer to go as an independent railroad by 1959, but the PHOEBE SNOW showed the pride of the railroad, still running its top train as a perfectly matched streamliner. *(J. J. Young)*

Above ▪ Eastbound #10 crossed the Chenango River in Binghamton in the summer of 1959. Number 10 was the NEW YORK MAIL, and was scheduled through Binghamton in darkness, so it must be running off schedule on this day. *(J. J. Young)*

New York State Branch Lines

Right ▪ The New York State branches of the Lackawanna are well known to the current generation of railfans, thanks to the New York, Susquehanna & Western, which acquired the lines from Conrail and operate them from Binghamton north to Utica and Syracuse. Central New York State is generally rural farming country, with handsome small towns and rich dairy farms dotting the hills and valleys of the region. The Lackawanna acquired the lines in the late 1800s to provide northern outlets for anthracite coal and other traffic moving to Lake Ontario or the large New York cities of Utica and Syracuse. The lines diverged at Chenango Forks, 11 miles north of Binghamton. The Utica line followed the valley of the Chenango River through some of the most beautiful scenery in New York, passing prosperous towns like Greene, Oxford, Norwich, and Sherburne on its 95-mile route. Near Greene, 19 miles north of Binghamton, a southbound freight is flying the white flags of an extra as its Mikado puts forth a massive pillar of smoke in the winter air. Snow on the ground is the norm for this cold and snowy part of the state; "white fertilizer," as the farmers call it, covers the ground usually from December to March. The Lackawanna did not have the valley of the Chenango to itself. The main line of the New York, Ontario & Western paralleled the Lackawanna along the Chenango between Norwich and Earlville. Greene played a role in the history of the Lackawanna. The Lackawanna was acquiring its lines north of Binghamton in the second half of the 1800s, with an eye to reaching such major markets as Syracuse, Utica, and Lake Ontario. It had control of the Syracuse & Binghamton and was gaining control of the Utica, Chenango & Susquehanna Valley, but the S&B and UC&SV lines had a short gap between Greene, at the south end of the Utica line, and the Syracuse line at Chenango Forks. The Greene Railroad was built with Lackawanna financing to fill the gap. In 1870 DL&W leased the two lines and operated them as part of the growing Lackawanna system. *(Mike Del Vecchio collection)*

Below ▪ At Brisben, 5.88 miles north of Greene, a northbound passenger local is heading toward Norwich and Utica in this undated shot.

(Mike Del Vecchio collection)

Left ▪ The easternmost branch of the Lackawanna in New York State was the Richfield Springs Branch. The line extended 21.76 miles from a connection with the Utica line at Richfield Junction to its namesake town in New York's Otsego County, not far from the famous community of Cooperstown. GP7 964, a freight unit with dynamic brakes, switched the feed mill at West Winfield, a little over 14 miles west of Richfield Springs, on October 21, 1960. This line was certainly one of the most remote outposts of the Lackawanna, nearly extending into the region served by the Delaware & Hudson in Upstate New York. In rich dairy country, it was sustained by agricultural traffic like feed for the mills like the one at West Winfield. It survived after the EL gave up on it, becoming the Central New York Railroad in the 1970s with a solid-blue RS3 for power. It lasted into the ownership of the Central New York by the Delaware Otsego Corporation, and is now abandoned.

(Charles Parsons collection)

Along the Susquehanna

Above ▪ At Binghamton, the Susquehanna River makes an almost 90 degree turn to the west, after heading compass north from Great Bend. The river valley is the natural pathway west, and both the Erie and the Lackawanna main lines followed it west as far as Waverly, where it again changes direction dramatically and turns to the south and east toward Wilkes-Barre. The Lackawanna followed the south bank of the river, the Erie the north. At Vestal, eight miles west of Binghamton, a westbound roustabout for Waverly was going into the siding by the depot, which illustrated the neo-Gothic Victorian style of the late 19th century with its steeply pitched roof and gingerbread details. It was May 25, 1959, and within a few months the Lackawanna trains would abandon these tracks and use the rival Erie's between Binghamton and Corning in a prelude to merger. The Lackawanna's Buffalo Division mainline was built in the early 1880s, and by the standards of the day was exceptionally well designed and constructed. On August 31, 1959, the last Lackawanna train used these tracks before the DL&W moved over to the Erie on the other side of the Susquehanna.

(Norman E. Kohl)

Right, Center ▪ The Susquehanna's deep blue waters are flowing west behind the Lackawanna tracks as a morning westbound freight passed west of Apalachin, New York behind the 604 leading a perfect A/B/A set of FTs. This snowy day is another testament to how winter holds its grip on Upstate New York, for the date of this wintry shot was April 9, 1956. *(Frank C. Kozempel)*

Right ▪ One of the dining car attendants is taking in the spring air as the eastbound PHOEBE SNOW barrels through Owego on May 26, 1959. The diner on the PHOEBE SNOW opened for lunch at Bath about an hour and a half earlier, so it's time for a break. At Owego, the Ithaca Branch of the Lackawanna crossed the Susquehanna River on a 1,080-foot, eight-span bridge and headed over to Ithaca, which it reached by switchbacks down the steep valley walls from East Ithaca. The branch saw its last train on May 25, 1957, and the bridge was torn down in 1959.

(Mike Del Vecchio collection)

Left - The scenic highlight of the Lackawanna in western New York was Dansville Hill. Eastbound trains faced a grade of 1.14% climbing out of the Genesee River watershed to the summit at Perkinsville. The grade led out of the Genesee watershed to the Cohocton Valley at Atlanta, and a relatively easy run to Bath and Corning following the path of the Cohocton. The PHOEBE SNOW was climbing the grade behind F3s in February 1950; it will be over a year before the E8s arrive to take their place on the train. The tracks cling to the hillside on a huge fill, with the fertile fields of the valley just out of sight to the left of the pole line.

(Paul Reynolds)

Left - An eastbound freight with a block of refrigerator cars bringing perishables east ascended the grade behind an A/B set of F7s in February 1950. The 634 A/B was part of the order for F7s in 1949 that completed the F unit fleet on the Lackawanna. Just two or three F units were needed on the Buffalo Division trains, but only with some assistance could they make it over Dansville Hill.

(Paul Reynolds)

Below - As the train plodded past, a howl of 567s in Run 8 echoed off the limestone bluffs as pushers 662 A/B assisted the eastbound freight up the hill. The photographer panned the shot slightly, with the nose of the 662 in perfect focus as the low-geared F3s do the job they were purchased to do, low speed lugging as pushers on the Lackawanna's toughest hills.

(Paul Reynolds)

Dansville & Mount Morris Connection

Right ■ The Dansville & Mount Morris was a 7.8-mile short line that connected the town of Dansville with the Lackawanna at Groveland, 68.3 miles east of Buffalo. The line had its headquarters at Dansville, where its cute little 2-6-0 565 was under steam in the early 1950s for photographer Bill Ellis. *(William Ellis)*

Below ■ In April 1951 the Lackawanna and D&MM are exchanging cars at the Groveland interchange. Pacific 1125 was assigned to the way freight, and its engineer is concentrating on the backup move as he leans out of the cab window, attired in the classic blue cap and denim jacket of steam railroaders. Most shots of the Lackawanna Pacifics in the 1950s are in New Jersey commuter service, so it's a bit of a surprise to be reminded that the engines also served the railroad in other capacities. The 1125 was not especially suited to freight work, having 79" drivers designed to propel it along at passenger-train speeds. *(Paul Reynolds)*

The 1125 moves around the lead track as the D&MM's Mogul 565 continues to switch the interchange at Groveland. *(Paul Reynolds)*

West to Buffalo

Above ▪ Richard Solomon was in the PHOEBE SNOW's square-ended Tavern Lounge car speeding east along the raceway on March 31, 1959 as #6 passed an eastbound freight on the triple track not far east of Buffalo. The freight has an interesting set of power, an A/B/B/A set of F3s, all in the now-standard former passenger scheme. The lead unit, the 802-A, was of course delivered in that scheme as one of the passenger units that, before the E8s arrived, would have been on the point of the PHOEBE. *(Richard Solomon)*

Above ▪ The eastbound PHOEBE SNOW had the usual two E8s on March 31, 1959, waiting for the passengers to load and the order to proceed east from Buffalo across the length of the Lackawanna to Hoboken. *(Richard Solomon)*

Farewell

Above ▪ It's hard to pick one scene to summarize a railroad as varied in its operations, geography, and motive power as the Lackawanna. But this scene of a 4-6-2 heading west under the catenary at East Orange, New Jersey on December 13, 1952 seems to sum up a good deal of the magic of the Lackawanna. The beautifully maintained tracks, the elevated right-of-way, speak to the pride and commitment to quality that characterized the Road of Phoebe Snow. A year after this shot was taken, there were no more Lackawanna steam engines sending their white columns of smoke skyward to be tinted by the last rays of a December sun. In less than a decade, the Lackawanna itself was gone, merged – some say submerged – in the marriage with the Erie. Change happens quickly on the railroad scene, and we are indebted to all the photographers who took the time and effort to wait alongside the Lackawanna to record scenes like this, scenes that we can relive through the legacy of